Whither Thou Goest?
You've Got to Be Kidding!

by Carolyn Gray Thornton

Copyright 2004 by Skyward Publishing, Inc.

Publisher: Skyward Publishing, Inc.
                  813 Michael Street
                  Kennett, Missouri 63857
                  E-mail: info@skywardpublishing.com
                  Web Site: www.skywardpublishing.com
                  Phone: 573-888-5026

First Printing 2004
Second Printing 2006

Library of Congress Cataloging-in-Publication Data

Thornton, Carolyn Gray, 1925-
    Whither thou goest? : you've got to be kidding! / by Carolyn Gray
Thornton ; edited by Charlotte Harris.
        p. cm.
    ISBN 1-881554-35-Xs (alk. paper)
    1. Thorton, Carolyn Gray, 1925—Humor. 2. Spouses of clergy—Humor.
3. Families of clergy—Humor. 4. Methodists—Humor. 5. United
Methodist Church (U.S.)—Clergy—Humor. I. Harris, Charlotte. II.
Title.
BX8495.T62 A3 2004
253' .22—dc22
                                                        2003022575

Printed in the United States of America
Cover Design by Angela Underwood
Website www.booksindesign.com

DEDICATION

To our grandchildren

Michael Patrick and William Lester Thornton

Penny Jean and Kevin Wayne Garnett

Christopher Wayne and Alison Lynn Aldridge and

Jonathan Mark Thornton

May your life journeys also bring you joy.

CONTENTS

Acknowledgment   iv
Foreword—by Lester I. Thornton   vi
Prologue   x

1.   *I Didn't Bargain for This*
Call Waiting   2
Message in Song   5
Prayers from the Heart   8
There's Comfort in Numbers   11
Let's Shake on It   14
We're Having a Party   16
Telephone Message Problems   18
Let the Little Children   21
Rumors Have a Life of Their Own   24
Time to Get Moving   27

2.   *I'm Doing My Best*
Trying Too Hard   30
Have You Been Pounded Yet?   33
Sights That Reveal   36
Testing, One, Two, Three, Testing   39
Dressing for Success   42
Marital Discord   45
Machines and Me   48
Highways to ????   50
The Imperfections of Being Perfect   53
Waitress Woes   55
Dusty Memories   57

3. Hey, I Think I'm Catching On

Cues from the Pews 62
Funeral Mishaps 65
More Funeral Mishaps 68
The Minister's Family Cat 70
Lighting One Little Candle 73
Basket Dinners 76
Responsibilities 79
Feeling Down in the Mouth? 82
Picture This 85
Lessons in Graciousness 88
Dream Along with Me 91
Highway Conversations
        Memories of Family Travels 94
What's That You Say? 97
Can You Hear Me Now? 100
I Didn't Catch the Name 103
Side Effects May Cause Vocabulary Lapses 106
Help Is Just a Phone Call Away 109
What's for Supper 113
Those Hazy, Lazy Days of Summer
        Bring Challenges 115
It's Easy to Get All Keyed Up These Days 118
Let Me Tell You 122
Giving Birth to Traditions 124

4. Look at Me Now!

A Community of Women 128
Career Roller Coaster Ride 131
First Sightings 134
Responsibilities Are Assigned
    for Various Reasons 137
What to Do with Extra Time Has Problems 140
VIPs Together 143
Thoughts on Making a List 145

5. It's a Good Life, Carolyn T.

Out to the Airport and Down the
        Roads to Grandmother's House We Go 150
Living in Mayberry,
        or Down the Road Suits Me Just Fine 154
Messages and Inspirations in the Church 157
Many Things Divide Us 160

Keep an Eye on Suspicious-Looking
    Little Old Ladies! 163
Do You Smell Something? 166
Auld Lang Syne 168
I Think I Am Learning to Like Spiders 171
I Will Be Walking My Body Back Home 175
What We Have Here Is a Surplus
    of Communication 178
Time to Come out of the Closet 181
Time and Tide Wait for No One 185
Mum's the Word When You Whisper a Message 188
Organizing Experiences Aren't Always Pleasant 191
Movie Going Brought Up to Date 195
Life's Paradoxes Hit at Any Age 199
A Daily Health Routine 203
Progress Is Wonderful, Once You Have
    Mastered It 206
Living with the Past in the Present 209

6. I Did It My Way

Friends and Neighbors 214
Precious Memories 216
Holiday Thoughts and Memories 218
How Do You Spell Relief? 222
Views from the Window 225
Telling the Stories Is Important 228
People Who Need People Are the
    Luckiest People 231
Memories Are Made from Such as This 235
Preachers' Kids 239
Our Children Speak for Themselves 242
I Was Stereotyped—by Michael H. Thornton 243
I Was Dealt a Double Whammy—by Shirley Garnett 245
Enriched by the Experience of Dad's Call—
    by Mark Thornton 247
Growing up P.K.—by Susan Thornton 252
I Belong 261

ACKNOWLEDGMENTS

I want to give special thanks to two people who have made it possible for this book to be a reality. They are my husband, Lester I. Thornton, and sister, Ellen Gray Massey. They helped greatly with the mechanics of getting the words in manuscript form, teaching me some tricks of the computer, and doing the tedious job of line editing. But their biggest help was in their constant support, encouragement, and praise. When I decided no one would want to read this, they convinced me that I was wrong. If I wasn't wrong, then you, the reader, will have to tell them. I don't have the heart to do it.

I also want to thank our four children—Michael, Shirley, Mark, and Susan—who joined me in this journey into parsonage life. They gave love, joy, fun, and excitement to the journey and provided lots of material to write about. They each have supported me in the task of writing my memories of that time with ideas, their own memories, and continued encouragement and interest.

The members of each of the churches and communities where we lived deserve gold stars for putting up with me and letting me feel that maybe I did belong.

And a special thanks goes to the women in the local, district, conference, and jurisdiction United Methodist Women who gave me opportunities I could have never imagined without them. Our shared purpose has been a highlight of my life.

FOREWORD

The author and I have had a very close relationship for more than fifty-five years. On our anniversary in 2004, we will have been married fifty-eight years. In those years, there was a brief time in military service. My *tux* for the wedding was the summer khaki uniform of the United States Army. Then came a year in college as I finished my degree. Carolyn had completed her degree just after our marriage and worked to help meet expenses.

After graduation I began a career in agricultural education. My first work was to reopen a vocational agriculture department, which had been closed for a lack of teachers since many were in branches of military service. Starting in mid-year, I completed three-and-one-half years then was employed by the University of Missouri in agricultural extension work. Moving in those early years prepared us for the later moves required in what is called *itinerant ministry*. My own experience in any form of church activity would not be called normal. Growing up in the hills of the Ozarks, there were not many of the *established churches*.

In our first experience with The Methodist Church, a Sunday School class needed a teacher. I discovered the *Church* was much more than I had known and began to feel a push toward ministry. We did not know much about what was required and with two children Carolyn felt, and I agreed, the idea did not seem practical. A professional move placed me in Carolyn's hometown and teaching a Sunday School class. Again, the *call to ministry* came, and we struggled with what that meant for us. Finally, with guidance from the former pastor, then a district superintendent, I *tested the waters* by filling in for pastors who needed someone to preach.

After several months, I finally decided the only way I could find out what God wanted was to try it. Carolyn asked why I couldn't serve part-time and continue my professional career with the better salary and retirement possibilities. Though she was not enthusiastic about my doing so, I accepted my first appointment and spent three years as a seminary student and student pastor. During that time, I was away from home for about half the week. She took care of the children, now up to three with another expected in about four months. Church details were often left up to her during the week and weekends were often spent with her typing my papers for seminary classes and helping prepare the bulletins for worship.

As a personal interest, she wrote skits and plays that could be done by children, women of the church, and in 4-H clubs. She also wrote a weekly column in the small newspaper in that community. Our first move took us to a larger community, more church responsibility. Now, with four children, she was under stress of responsibilities as mother, pastor's wife, and resident of the community. She also worked as a child welfare worker and as a local newswriter with a radio station. She began writing columns about the pressures brought by these tasks and titled them "Caught In The Middle."

After retirement, she continued to write about her experiences and, now being older, describes "The Joys of Middle Age Plus."

It is out of that experience and the chaos that sometimes happened that she wrote columns in a weekly, and later a daily, paper that continued to bring comments of appreciation from those who read her musings about life.

Though I admit to being prejudiced, it has been amazing to me to hear people comment about the joy they got from reading her columns. Her memories reminded others of their own and brought chuckles, belly laughs, and, occasionally tears. It has been my pleasure to take many calls for her and report that "so and so" called and wanted her to know how much they appreciated this week's writing. My own evaluation that her writing was worthy of publication in a book has been bolstered by the comments others have made to her. I continue to be amazed that she has been able to touch the lives of many individuals and bring insight, joy, and understanding as her descriptions make their *ordinary* living become extraordinary.

Reading these snapshots of life will enable you to journey with her, see how much she has grown, and find hope and joy in your own living. As wife, mother, pastor's wife, and in the many capacities I have observed in her, she has exhibited many good qualities and has brought wisdom, wit, insight, joy, and faith to me, our children, our extended family, and to the many relationships she has developed with so many individuals.

Lester I. Thornton, Retired United Methodist Minister

PROLOGUE

Each day that I live brings more memories of each period in my life. I have been privileged to have two books published that gave me opportunities to reflect on my senior status while looking back to nostalgic memories of my childhood. These books, *A Funny Thing Happened on the Road to Senility* and *For Everything There Is a Season* stress the benefits of being what I call Middle Age Plus, the time of life past middle age that has many pluses other ages do not.

But these books leave out a very important segment of my life. That segment is the time when our children were all at home and I was dealing with the daily problems of a wife, mother, and career with another large identification. I had become *A Minister's Wife*. This happened to me midway through my adult years, and the adjustment for me and the children had some rocky moments as well as some wonderful times.

This book shares my story as I went from a woman who *knew* she was not cut out to be a minister's wife to one who became comfortable in the role. Since I am now Middle Age Plus, the stories are told through the perspective of my present age. But my memory is still good, and I don't think I have put too rosy a glow on my life.

The essays took place in the western half of Missouri, mainly in small towns up and down the Kansas line. But they could have been written about your town or your church. Even if you are not a United Methodist, you will find experiences you can relate to.

So let's share some laughs, some tears, and mainly some smiles as we join in helping me find my way as a Minister's Wife.

I DIDN'T BARGAIN FOR THIS

Plans ready for the future,
Our lifetime dreams secure
Were tossed aside in chaos
To follow God's detour.

CALL WAITING

My husband, Lester, and I were in bed one night in the early 1950s when he surprised me by saying, "Carolyn, I have been thinking that maybe I should become a minister." We had two children, ages three and one, had just bought a farm, and were finishing a remodeling job on the house that had been started before we bought the place. Lester was the county extension agent for Cedar County, Missouri. We had recently joined The Methodist Church in Stockton, the county seat, and attended fairly regularly. In fact, Lester had begun to teach an adult Sunday School class. I helped in the nursery some and had been a teacher at the Vacation Bible School. But our church life was not a very big part of our life then. Or I thought it wasn't.

I was so unprepared for his remark that I answered, "Good. Then after that you can become a trapeze artist." I did not think he was serious and I spontaneously thought of another thing that seemed just as unlikely. He became very silent and I realized he wasn't kidding. He did not mention the idea again to me for several years. I never brought it up again either, because I certainly did not want to be a minister's wife.

In the meantime, we had moved to Vernon County and had bought eighty acres of my parents' farm and had settled as neighbors to my parents. We had a third child, and Lester continued in agriculture extension work in my home county.

I thought he had dismissed the notion as I became more and more involved in the care of my parents who were in their eighties. The children were in a rural school, active in 4-H, and I thought we were settled for life.

Not so. Lester continued to be very active in the church, now in Nevada, Missouri, and again brought up the thought that he should go into the ministry. Hoping to dissuade him, I went with him to talk with our friend and former pastor, Ed Neimeyer, who was now the district superintendent of our church's district. More conversations followed as I expressed my doubts to Ed and his wife, Henrietta, who listened and understood my reluctance.

My parents needed me to be nearby. We could not afford to give up the good salary, benefits, and retirement security that the job with the University Extension Service offered. Lester would have to go three years to seminary, which was an additional cost. As a final deterrent, I had become pregnant again. I thought that surely would be the deciding factor.

But it wasn't. Discussions continued, opportunities to preach as a guest speaker were offered. I had to admit that he did a good job with those first sermons. But that wasn't what bothered me. I knew by now that he would be a good minister. What I also knew was that I wasn't cut out to be a minister's wife.

However, the decision was made, and Lester was appointed to be the minister at Archie, Missouri, which was about an hour's drive away from my parents, our farm, and the future I had thought was secure.

I knew that to save our marriage I would need to be a good sport and go along with the plans. We visited the church, supposedly anonymously, one Sunday before it was time to move. I had to admit that I liked the people and the town. But I knew I could not fill the role they were expecting in their minister's wife.

We kept our farm, rented our house, and got our things ready for the move. In June 1962, we followed the stock truck, which was loaded with our furniture, up Highway 71 to begin our new life. I tried to keep the kids from seeing that I was crying.

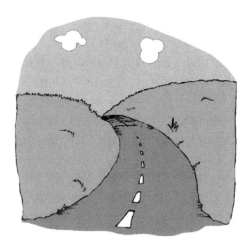

MESSAGE IN SONG

I recently attended a retreat for United Methodist Women. It was very pleasurable. I had fun, learned a lot, and came home with enthusiasm. I was ready to roll up my sleeves and work even harder to reach the goals of the organization. As I was returning home, I began thinking about how different this was to the first retreat I attended after I became a minister's wife. (You realize I had already been a soldier's wife, a student's wife, a teacher's wife, and a county agent's wife—all the same man. But now suddenly I was a minister's wife—still the same man.)

I was not enthused about my role and was sure I was unsuited for the position. I was embarking on a new way of life with much trepidation. Another minister's wife who had been a friend for several years told me that going to this retreat would make me feel more secure, so I reluctantly left our infant daughter and other three children with my husband for this overnight retreat at a rustic camp.

It was late September, and the camp was in the Ozarks so we were scheduled to see beautiful foliage that would add to the spiritual benefits of the gathering. The cabins were unheated, but September was supposed to be warm enough for comfortable sleeping in our bedrolls.

A woman who felt strongly that silence and meditation were very important had planned the retreat. Before the required silence periods we had several small group discussions with other wives. I suppose we were given a subject to discuss. All I know is, I was put in with a group of women who sensed my feelings of insecurity, and they did their best to set me at ease. Their way of setting me at ease put me on edge even more. They were strong believers in hearing the voice of God daily telling them what to do.

I made the mistake of asking how they knew it was the voice of God talking to them instead of their own wishes or ideas. That released a torrent of well-meaning words of advice, prayers for my ability to discern, and stories telling me about their own experiences with the voice of God.

I wanted to crawl into a hole and disappear, but this wasn't possible. I wasn't left alone a minute. There was always some older woman with her arm around me counseling me on my spiritual growth. Thankfully dinner and a group worship service and singing interrupted these actions. I found one other woman I knew slightly, but I didn't have time to tell her my situation before we were whisked off to our cabins with the admonition that, after the bell rang in a few minutes, we were not to speak until morning. Then we would join at the outdoor auditorium for morning worship.

These cabins had eight bunk beds, walls, and a ceiling. The plumbing was down the hill in a lighted bathhouse. As soon as the sun went down, a breeze came up and the area became very chilly. No, it wasn't chilly. It was downright cold. I quickly did what was necessary at the bathhouse before trying to scurry into my sleeping bag. One of my cabin mates drew me aside and said, "Now, Carolyn, when you go to bed, empty your mind of everything, relax, and pray that during the night you will hear the voice of God. It may be just a word, it might be a song, or it might be more. But follow my advice and you will get a message." Then the bell rang.

I hurried to get into the sleeping bag but soon realized the bag would not ward off the cold. I got up and put on all my clothes over my pajamas and got back into the bed. I still was cold but couldn't do anything more about it, so I tried to relax.

I thought, *Well, I am in this situation. I might as well follow the woman's directions.* I couldn't do much else. We just had to lie quietly frozen and be spiritual.

I remembered her words, "Relax, empty your mind, sleep, and wait for your message." I never did relax. It was way too cold for that. But I did eventually sleep.

And sure enough, in the middle of the night, I woke up with a popular nonsense song running through my head. "I'm Henry the Eighth I am, Henry the Eighth I am, I am."

So if this was my message from God, I realized the message must be to keep a sense of humor and laugh. I sat up in the cold bunk and stifled my giggles. I was ready for the morning now.

PRAYERS FROM THE HEART

I have never liked to pray in public. That is, when I am praying for the public, I tend to make speeches rather than pray. I notice this in other people's prayers also. One glaring example of this was when a visiting minister was asked to have the benediction. His prayer included an upcoming event he prayed for. He not only prayed for the success of the event but he gave the time, place, and date just in case God hadn't heard all about it. Obviously, his prayer was aimed at potential attendees.

Many times, in spite of my reluctance, I have been called upon to give a prayer, often without warning. It seems that people think because I am the wife of a minister, I should have prayers, scriptures, and meditations ready at a moment's notice. What's more, I should be happy to share these gifts often. Maybe I should be, but I am not. I can prepare a meditation fairly easily, but I want to prepare it, not just come up with some trite sayings and verses. I do know a few scriptures, but unless they are very well-known, I couldn't give you chapter and verse on them. At one time my sons found a scripture in the King James Version of the Bible that they delighted in. It was directed to those who pisseth against the wall. For a while I could remember where to find that, but I am afraid I no longer remember that bit of enlightenment either.

My challenge to those who expect me to be a font of spiritual blessings is, "Do you expect your doctor's wife to be able to operate on your brain?" One friend countered with the idea that in an emergency perhaps the doctor's wife would know more about medicine than the average person would.

I have, at times, managed to come forth with an acceptable prayer, especially if I am given a little notice. I do feel hypocritical when giving it, however. I am more aware of what the audience thinks about it than I am concerned about God's response.

Except when using the Lord's Prayer, I never begin a prayer with "Our Father." Instead I prefer to use the salutation of "Creator God." To me it encompasses more of the greatness and wonder of God.

Lester was a layman in our present church before he became a minister. He was on the planning committee for the present church building, and we were still members here when it was completed and we moved from the historic downtown structure to the imposing new brick one. Then, at the fifth year anniversary of this event, the congregation had a celebration. Lester was invited back to deliver the sermon as a *local boy made good*. He did a fine job, of course. A retired minister who had previously served this church then was asked to give the benediction. In this prayer, the beloved former pastor made a mini-sermon on the same scripture Lester had used, putting in the points he thought should have been stressed. Lester had been coming from a different approach, but in this more than five-minute benediction prayer, we heard the sermon again from the older man's standpoint. Our necks got a little stiff from bowing that long.

Which brings up another subject. I don't like it when I am told by a minister—or anyone leading a service—to close my eyes and bow my head in prayer. Maybe I would rather pray looking up with my eyes wide open. I'll admit it would be rather conspicuous in a church service, but no one would see me because everyone else should be having their eyes closed and their head bowed, shouldn't they?

My first experience with taking communion from a common cup (remember United Methodists only use grape juice) included each of the persons in the circle giving a sentence prayer prior to taking the cup. I said something like, "Help us learn to be helpful to others" or something broad and meaningless. But my real prayer as I received the cup was, "Please, God, don't let me throw up before this thing is over!"

THERE'S COMFORT IN NUMBERS

Very early in my life as a wife of a minister I discovered that even though I felt like a misfit, there were others who shared some of my feelings. I was blessed with being in a district where there was a very active group of ministers' wives. We were called the Susanna Wesleys. At that time there were no male spouses of ministers in our rural area close to Kansas City. This location made it possible for student ministers who were attending Saint Paul School of Theology in Kansas City to serve the churches in our district and drive to the seminary on Tuesday morning and return Friday afternoon. Therefore most of the women left to take care of things at home and in the churches were young wives, many with small children.

Our group met once a month in each other's parsonages, usually for an all day meeting during the week when many of the husbands were gone. We would carpool, in the days before car seats were heard of for children, with three or four women and up to five or six babies and toddlers in laps.

The conversation on these trips was jolly and open. We discussed everything from childcare to how to deal with some church members who had been critical. We had programs that were fun and meaningful, but we stayed away from the "How to Be a Good Minister's Wife" topics.

I soon learned that I wasn't the only one in the group who did not feel fulfilled with constant meditations and spiritual advice. We formed some strong friendships that exist today, some forty years later.

One of the fun things we did was to put on an operetta at the Wives' Tea at Annual Conference. We changed words to the tunes from Mary Poppins and poked fun at the various types of wives we had encountered. The characters were given names like Pietistic Paula, Martyr Mary, and Subservient Sue. We had a ball rehearsing the show and were looking forward to presenting it at the tea.

It happened that a very serious subject was being discussed on the floor of the conference and when the bishop's wife came to give us greetings, she chided us gently for not being on the floor listening to our husbands' discussions instead of having this play.

I had spent many hours on the floor of the conference listening to debates, but in that setting, that year, the wives had to either sit in the bleachers of a field house or in folding chairs at the back of the room. We had no voice or vote and our presence was usually only observed with a complimentary remark from the bishop immediately before we left for the tea. I felt that we were doing more good for our cause by giving us a chance to laugh at ourselves and share together than being mere spectators to our husbands' debates.

In later years, I found my support group through the members of the district and conference United Methodist Women. The wives' groups had diminished to a few semiformal occasions a year, since most of the women were now employed outside the home. In the United Methodist Women, I was able to be one of the crowd but still very involved. Here I had both voice and vote and was able to exert leadership and give strength to the Mission Purpose of the United Methodist Women. And we still had fun and laughed at ourselves while taking our roles very seriously.

I have often wondered how my years as a preacher's spouse would have turned out if I hadn't had the support of these two groups of women. Maybe the two organizations would have thrived better without me, but I doubt that I would have managed without them.

LET'S SHAKE ON THAT

The most criticism I ever received on my performance as a minister's wife had to do with greeting people at the back of the church after the service was over. In some churches, I was expected to go back and stand by my husband as he shook hands with the members as they left the sanctuary. I could see absolutely no reason for me to do this. I was not the one who had preached the sermon. All I had done was to hold an infant, a wiggling toddler, and give the evil eye to older children who were making noise. That didn't call for a receiving line.

I argued that you didn't expect the wife of the school principal to stand by him as he was giving out diplomas. The doctor's wife didn't come with him when he came to the waiting room to give news of their sick one. The lawyer's wife didn't stand with her husband before the judge at the end of the trial. So why should I traipse back to the rear to shake everyone's hand as they left the church?

I was told that they wanted to see me. Well, there I was, right in the midst of them where I belonged. They could see me there. I wasn't hiding.

I always stood around visiting after the service. It wasn't like I bolted for the backdoor the minute the last amen was sung. But many people told me that other wives had always gone with their husbands to the door.

This is one way I decided I wasn't like the other wives. This was Lester's show, not mine. There was more reason for the choir director, organist, or candlelighters to line up with him than for me to do so.

I decided it was a throwback to the feeling that you *hire* the minister, but you *get* the minister's wife also. Even though I was trying to live up to expectations to make it easier on Lester, this was one that I passed on.

I had a good excuse at first. I was six months pregnant when we first arrived at the first church. And then in the fall I had the baby to hold. Neither of these things worked well with standing in line with one hand free for greeting people.

However, after the baby was old enough to be on her own, I lost that excuse, but by then I decided I didn't need an excuse. I just didn't see the need for doing that.

I mentioned this at a meeting of other ministers' wives and some of them were very surprised at my reaction. One said it was a time she looked forward to.

I was happy for her.

WE'RE HAVING A PARTY

During the years I was a minister's wife we were invited to many homes for dinner. Often couples having a golden wedding celebration would include us in the guest list. Of course, I was also usually included in the rehearsal dinners when Lester was performing a wedding ceremony. Many times, when we went to pay our bill at the cash register when eating out after church services someone had already paid for our meal.

After we retired back to Nevada, the current minister and his wife, who had been long time clergy friends, were taking us out to dinner at a local restaurant. A local businessman, who had known us for years and was a member of the Nevada church, picked up the tab for all of us. (We told our friends that they still owed us a dinner!)

We were included in receptions for high-school graduates who were members of the church and, of course, for the family dinners the church served following a funeral.

These special times meant a lot to each of us, and we enjoyed being with the church members in these more social times. But not many people invited us to a purely social party. At first I was hurt by this exclusion because often the party would be discussed in my presence, but we were not invited to attend. It was as if no one would even expect the minister and his wife to come to *just* a party that wasn't connected to the church in some way. At times I suspected it was because they didn't want the minister there to see that they were serving liquor. Other times I was sure that they thought our presence would throw a pall on the activities. They probably thought that we certainly couldn't be any fun or add to the festivities in any way.

There were several big exceptions to this. Families who had children the same age as ours often included us in their family fun times, but not in purely adult activities.

One of our last churches was a surprise to us because we were included in many social events. Following a church board meeting that didn't last too long, one of the members would say, "Come on over to our house and we'll play pitch for a while." And we would do it and have a great time. Some of the women would ask me to come along on a shopping trip or just to go out for lunch for the fun of it. I imagine the fact that this was the first time we had come to a church without some of our children still living at home with us could have been part of the reason. But I suspect it had more to do with the nature of the people in that church, plus the fact that Lester and I had relaxed in our *roles* enough that we were seen as people and not as the minister and his wife.

Now that we have retired, we seem to be too busy to enjoy many social activities with friends in the neighborhood or with folks in town. I want to do something to correct that, so I am considering having a little card party this summer. I wonder if I should invite the new minister. Oh, he's probably too busy to come to something like that, don't you think?

TELEPHONE MESSAGE PROBLEMS

I have enjoyed using the telephone ever since I was a small child. At our farm home I would climb onto the kitchen stool to crank the correct number of rings on the old party line to call my friend. In Washington, D.C. in the wintertime I would get a tight hold on the tall-stemmed telephone with the ear receiver hanging on the side and ask for the number of my friend up the street. Later I learned to use the dial phone and now the touch-tone models. This expertise did not help me, however, in our first parsonage.

Lester was attending seminary in Kansas City from Tuesday morning to Friday noon. With the four children, I was left at home—the person that members of the congregation could call for information or to give a message to Lester. Every other week Lester drove a carpool to the city and I was left with no *wheels* except my trusty bicycle. That didn't work too well with an infant daughter to take with me. I usually walked wherever I needed to go in this little town, or I sent the older children on their bikes for groceries or to take messages. It was a very friendly, safe town and my neighbors were very good to me when I needed more help than the children could provide. Often I would get calls asking if I needed anything.

The phone system in this little town served both this town and the slightly larger town about five miles away. The phone book, therefore, served both towns.

I was adjusting to this new life as a minister's wife with a newborn child plus another just starting school and two older school-age children. I was not comfortable in this role, but I was trying very hard to do what was expected of me.

One day while feeding Susan I got a phone call that really shook me up. A man on the other end of the line identified himself, but I didn't recognize the name. That was not surprising since I hadn't learned many of the names in our new town. But what he said shook me up. He said, "This is Joe Owsley (obviously not his name since I can't remember the real one anyway), I wanted to know what time I should come pray with you." Now I said that the people in town were helpful and concerned about my well-being, but come pray with me? I tried frantically to think what I should say. I think I said something about the fact that I was giving my daughter a bottle right now. He replied that wouldn't be any problem if the door were unlocked. I became even more alarmed but didn't want to create an incident. I asked if he would be coming alone. He then seemed to be confused also and said he thought there would be a partner waiting for him at the church.

That cleared the air a little. At least he was not planning to come to the house to pray with *me*! As I was heaving a sigh of relief, he said, "Shirley, I hate to bother you, but I lost my sheet giving the schedule of the prayers." Shirley! That was the name of the minister's wife in the adjoining town. He had called the number identifying the Methodist parsonage, not noticing that the prefix for the number was not for his town. I then found out that the neighboring church was having a twenty-four-hour prayer vigil in preparation for a revival. That minister was also gone to seminary during the week, and Shirley was left in charge the same as I was. She also had a new baby, so the poor man had no clue to the fact that he had contacted a greenhorn in the business instead of the organized Shirley.

Another time in this same location, I received a call while Lester was away at seminary. A very familiar voice in a slow drawl said, "Hello, Carolyn. Is Lester handy?" Thinking I knew that the man who was calling was a new friend who often teased me, I replied, using the same slow drawl, "Well, sometimes he's handy and sometimes he's not very handy." There was a pause at the other end of the line, and then the man continued, "This is Richard Dork of the funeral home. I wanted Lester to know that Mrs. Jones has died." I quickly switched to a more professional tone and told him I would contact my husband and have him return the call. Then I sat down and couldn't decide whether to laugh or cry.

Maybe in this case I should have done like the operators tell us so often today, "If you want to make a call, please hang up and try again." Maybe I would have done better a second time.

LET THE LITTLE CHILDREN

Kids in church can be a source of amusement or irritation. Much of it depends on whether it is your kids or someone else's. However, after the service is over, sometimes whatever happened can more than make up for any embarrassment by the fun of telling about it afterwards.

In one of Lester's first churches, the floor was slanted toward the front of the sanctuary and the carpet just covered the aisle, the foyer, and the altar area. On one rainy Sunday, a bored child took a package of ball bearings out of his pocket to look at them. His mother was shocked to see that he had brought them with him and started to take them from him. Of course, her preventive action actually started the ball rolling, literally. As she reached to take the package from her son, he dropped the entire bundle and the ball bearings hit the wooden floor with a crash that startled everyone in the church. Then they started rolling slowly toward the front. A few people tried to catch some of the ball bearings or stop the rolling action with their feet, but a few of them got lodged behind the supports for the pews or women's purses. Naturally, they moved away from their resting places at various times during the service so that every prayer, song, or point of the sermon was accompanied by the sound of rolling balls on the wooden floor. The mother insisted that there were only about twelve of the little culprits in her son's pocket to begin with, but each of the twelve had at least seven lives. Thankfully, most of the congregation enjoyed the diversion and sympathized with the mother.

At another church, the neighbor of a child was not as forgiving. A two-year-old girl had come to church with brand new patent leather shoes. She was very proud of her new shoes and was showing them to everyone she met. When the service started, she was seated in the pew by her mother, but she continued to be mesmerized by her shoes. She began swinging her little feet back and forth to let the light from the ceiling reflect on the shiny surface. Unfortunately, her feet kept hitting the back of the pew ahead of her. The woman who was seated in that pew endured about as much of the commotion as she could stand before turning around and scolding the child. This upset the mother who had not been aware that the child's actions were annoying. Those seated in that section of the church were either annoyed at the child and her mother or annoyed at the woman who had turned to correct the child. A happy little incident that turned sour spoiled the morning for several people.

Each of these children is now a grown adult. The boy is still active in the same congregation, and he often hears the story retold about the sound effects he created years ago. Incidentally, the church now has a rug over *all* the sanctuary floor.

The little girl is active in a church, but, unfortunately, not in the one where she wore her pretty new shoes. The family left that congregation soon after this incident happened. I wonder if she remembers the day her joy over her new shoes turned to tears over being scolded by a stranger.

We each can put ourselves either in the place of the mother or the woman in the pew in front of the family. From a distance of years, our middle age plus wisdom says we would have celebrated with the child. But maybe not if we had an aching back, were hard of hearing, and the noise kept us from hearing the service, or if we were facing a hard problem, and we really needed the quiet of the service to help reach a solution.

Isn't it easy to judge others?

RUMORS HAVE A LIFE OF THEIR OWN

One of the things that plague parsonage families is the tendency of people everywhere to love a bit of juicy gossip. Many a minister has had his career ruined by false rumors and gossip. We escaped most of that, thankfully, but there were a few exceptions.

One rumor I squelched before it began. However, knowing the kind lady involved, she probably would have kept it to herself if I hadn't clarified the situation.

Our first parsonage was quite small and, as we had four children, the bedrooms were full. In order to have guests overnight we had a daybed in the living room that converted into a couch. A bus line that had one bus that arrived late at night, or really very early in the morning, served our town. When my brother Harold visited us, arriving by bus, we put him to bed on the living room daybed. We tried to keep quiet the next morning to let him sleep late. I kept the drapes closed, and the kids were quiet as they left for school.

About nine o'clock a friend from the congregation came to the door, bringing a jar of pickles for our daughter Shirley. We had been guests at her home earlier that week, and Shirley had asked for seconds and thirds of the sweet pickles on the table. This pleased the two ladies who were our hostesses, so one of them was bringing Shirley her own jar. She also brought a jar of apple butter they had just made.

I asked her in and she stepped inside the front door for a minute but said she was in a hurry to get to the post office. I was speaking in whispers and she followed suit in low tones, but she left very soon. After she had gone down the sidewalk, I turned to put the jars down, noticed Harold stirring a little, and realized with a start that I hadn't explained my whispers or the presence of a man sleeping in our living room. (This was during the week when Lester was away at the seminary.)

I hurried to the door and called out to her, "Thanks again for this apple butter. My brother who is visiting really loves apple butter, and he will enjoy it with his breakfast." Our visitor seemed very relieved to know who my guest was. I went on to explain that he had come in on the bus from Kansas City, and I was hoping he could sleep a little longer. Although I doubt that she would have wondered about the situation to anyone else, I was very glad I squelched that rumor before it got started.

At another church quite a few years later, I started a rumor when my sister Ellen and I took a trip back to Washington to see our relatives and Lester stayed behind. We had just moved to this appointment and he didn't feel it would be good for him to be gone the two weeks we had planned for our trip. Ellen was a teacher and needed to take such trips in the summer and, as we had just moved, I didn't have a new job to tie me down, so we left shortly after Lester and I got settled in the new parsonage. I heard later that the members of the congregation thought that Lester and I were having problems. A few weeks after we returned, one person told me he was so glad to see Lester and me on good terms because they were afraid they had a problem marriage to deal with.

Since we always got a good dose of stories about the families that had preceded us in each place, I am sure there were other rumors, exaggerated stories, and just plain gossip about us after we left. But only one was potentially harmful.

Before Lester became a minister, a co-worker was involved in an affair that got hushed up quickly. Several years later a friend of ours was told that the reason Lester went into the ministry was that I had threatened to leave him after I discovered an affair unless he would go into the ministry. Since I didn't even want him to become a preacher and he hadn't had an affair, the story was completely false, but it must have lingered on in the minds of some. Someone had obviously confused him with the other man and the story grew from there.

Gossip is very unkind. I never pass on such stories except to closest friends. And they always promise never to tell anyone else—except their closest friends.

TIME TO GET MOVING

Moving day! What a mixture of sadness, excitement, pandemonium, and fatigue comes with that term. In The United Methodist Church, there is a prescribed moving day for every minister who is being appointed to a new charge following the annual conference. This is necessary so that there will be an empty parsonage awaiting the new family. An early moving date can only be possible if there is a relative the *old* family can stay with or if someone can afford a few nights in a motel.

Often the moving van was loaded the day before the actual move. The family either camped out in the empty parsonage or stayed with some friends overnight. A frantic time of house-cleaning followed. No wife wanted the new folks to find dirt in the windowsills, grease on the stove hood, or bugs in the ceiling light fixtures.

The next morning the family, with pets, some fragile plants, and overnight luggage, loaded in the car to start to their new home. Very soon the new family arrived with their moving van full of furniture and started getting settled in.

It didn't always work that smoothly. One time the schedule called for our things to be loaded in the early morning, anticipating the new family's arrival after noon. Our van came as expected. We were busily loading it when the new family's van arrived mid-morning. Though we protested to the company that they weren't to come until after noon, they insisted they had to unload immediately to meet another scheduled pickup.

Hurrying back to our van, I discovered that the men were loading the new family's stuff into our van. It took all members of both families to clarify whose stuff belonged where. To add to the confusion, the kids from the new family, in their excitement of exploring their new home, opened the door to the study where we had secured our dog and cat in the emptied-out room. By now these pets were frantic because of the turmoil. The dog ran off through the park. Maxi went up a tree. Later we were able to get the cat down in time for the move, but we had to leave Toby. Our married daughter, Shirley, promised to keep checking until he returned and keep him for us until someone came up for a visit.

When we did leave, Michael, recently home from Vietnam, was with Lester in his loaded-down pickup. Our younger son, Mark, drove the family car that was loaded to the top in the rear seat. Susan and Maxi rode on top of the clothes in the back. I was balancing some potted plants between my feet in the passenger seat. We left Shirley holding eight-month-old granddaughter, Penny, standing by the driveway waving goodbye. It was the first time she hadn't moved with us. Our sons were going along only to help in the moving and would be returning to Butler. It was one of the saddest moves I made because it was changing us from a family of six to just Lester, Susan, and me.

The next time we moved, we had only Maxi to make the move with us.

2

I'M DOING MY BEST

This may not be my calling
But I cannot step aside.
If it'll keep us all from falling,
I'll do my best, with pride.

TRYING TOO HARD

One of the benefits I have received from our years of being active in the church is the joy of knowing people of different cultures, races, economic levels, and ages. Very early in Lester's ministry, The Methodist Church did away with the separate conference for the black churches. When he was in seminary in Kansas City, several of his classmates were black students, serving small black churches within driving distance of the city.

The vote was planned to take place at Annual Conference, but before that time many ministers were preparing their congregations so that they could be informed voters. Lester invited one of his friends to come for an evening service at our church, and I had invited him to come earlier to have dinner with us.

This parsonage was quite small with no dining room. We ate in the kitchen and had entertained the district superintendent and other visiting ministers there along with our family of four children. But I became worried that our guest might feel that we were not honoring him if we fed him in the kitchen. I began figuring out ways to move a table into the living room so that we could be more elegant. If we did this, there would not be room to sit around and visit before the meal and, with our active children, I was concerned that it would be a circus with people trying to move around. There was no restaurant in town that we could take our friend to (and if there had been at that time, it might have caused a bigger problem for him and us).

Lester heard me trying to decide what to do and quietly said to me, "If you are going to accept 'Charles' as an equal, then you need to treat him just as you would anyone else. You are putting obstacles in our path to friendship." I agreed. We ate in the kitchen and had a good time together. The white congregation said that after the first few words, they no longer were concerned that he was a black man preaching in their pulpit.

When I became active in the United Methodist Women in the South Central jurisdiction, I had the privilege of working on committees, traveling, sharing rooms, and having fun with Hispanic, Native American, and African-American women. Our friendship and respect for one another was a gift I will always cherish.

The officers on the jurisdiction level often visited other conferences in the jurisdiction to get better acquainted. Once when one of my friends was visiting our conference, I could not meet her at the airport because of other responsibilities. Another minister's wife offered to meet her and bring her to the meeting. Since she did not know the visiting friend, I described her. "She is about my size, dresses very stylishly, and has outstandingly beautiful eyes."

When the two arrived at the meeting, my local friend took me aside and said, "Carolyn, why on earth didn't you tell me she was black?" I was astonished to realize that I hadn't even thought about that when I was describing her. I was proud that race no longer was a distinguishing feature in our friendship. But I do realize it would have made it easier to identify my friend quickly.

HAVE YOU BEEN POUNDED YET?

We moved to a new parsonage in June right after our son Mark graduated from high school. For the first time we were a family with only one child as Mark stayed with Michael at our former location to continue his job there. Shirley was married and the mother of eight-month-old Penny. It was a traumatic time for us. We were leaving three of our children, our first grandchild, and moving three hours away.

Susan had been in a group of children in our immediate neighborhood and enjoyed constant playmates at any hour she chose. In the new location there were not many children evident at first glance. The ones in the new church lived on the other side of town from the parsonage. She was having a hard time adapting to this situation. I was not doing a whole lot better. I loved the people in our former church and left friends throughout the county and a job I liked. But most of all, I was having a hard time being so far from the other children.

Lester was the director of a four-church parish. Another minister shared the responsibilities of serving the four congregations—two in a small town about five miles away from our parsonage. The other minister and his family lived in this small town in another parsonage.

The other wife was very helpful in getting us information about the two towns and the people in the churches.

We were visiting on the phone about the smallest of the churches when she shocked me by asking, "Have they pounded you yet?" I stammered a reply that no—they had been very nice to us. Gloria hung up then to tend to her cooking and left me puzzling what she could be talking about.

I didn't mention the conversation to either Lester or Susan because I didn't want to cause them to be concerned. I could hardly hide my apprehension, however, when Lester came home and said that we were invited to the Amazonia United Methodist Church for a potluck supper. I wasn't supposed to take anything since we were the guests of honor.

As we drove the five hilly miles to Amazonia, I tried to imagine what Gloria meant by them pounding us. Was it some sort of initiation? I didn't think so because many of the members were senior citizens. Perhaps they would spend some time impressing us with their expectations, you know, pound in their ideas to us. That didn't sound right either.

We arrived at the church and went down to the basement for the lavish meal the ladies prepared. Since everything was very pleasant, I almost forgot my apprehension as I visited with the women and watched Lester visiting across the room with the men. Susan found Gloria's daughter, and they were having a good time comparing thoughts about school.

As the women were putting away the dishes and packing up their leftovers to take home, they pulled a tablecloth from a table in the corner that had covered numerous sacks and boxes.

The president of the United Methodist Women announced to everyone that they were ready for the pounding.

My heart was pounding with some apprehension as to what was expected of me, but I didn't see anything else that looked frightening. We were escorted to the table where we were shown the welcoming gifts. People had brought a pound of this and a pound of that for us to take back to our pantry. The dreaded pounding gave us sugar, home canned fruits and vegetables, jellies, meat, and baked goods.

Well, my children weren't living any closer than before, I didn't have a new job, Susan hadn't met many new friends, but at least I didn't have to worry about some mysterious rite of pounding. Instead we feasted well for quite a few days and realized that time would take care of some of our other concerns.

SIGHTS THAT REVEAL

When we were living in our second parsonage at Butler, Missouri, I read an article by a famous interior decorator. She said that the first thing a person sees upon entering your house should reflect the theme of the entire house and the family that lives there. Since I was going to have the trustees over to look into putting a shower in the basement for the boys, I thought maybe I should test out this theory.

I stood in the front door as if I were a stranger, assessing what I saw. The house was built so that part of the living room and all of the dining room was visible from the front door. Okay, what could I see? Well, I could see the piano, which is good. We do like music. But on the piano were stacks of music and hymnbooks in a rather untidy heap. Also there was a leftover Halloween decoration, three letters to be mailed by the next person going to town, a football, and an empty baby bottle with residue of milk still visible. The piano bench held Susan's trumpet case and music as well as the denim jacket she wore home from school. These things certainly set the theme all right. But this first and last resting place for articles inside the front door shouldn't be completely uncluttered or a visitor would not be aware that we were a busy family. A few changes there and I could feel fairly comfortable with the view.

I looked farther on. There stood the tall bookcase Michael had built in shop with the encyclopedia set neatly lined up inside. Of course, the fifth volume was first and the first volume fifth, but that just showed that they had been used at least once. On top of the bookcase was a picture of Susan, a book that wouldn't fit inside the bookcase, and a candle. (Well, really, if you got up real close you could see the button that fell off Lester's shirt a week ago, two paper clips, a key for something that we can't remember, and two diaper pins.) You can't see these things from the front door, however, so they don't count.

I felt pretty good about this view. It shows we can read. It shows we are proud of our children, and it shows that we have more books than we have room for.

So now I look into the dining room. That is something else! There in the middle of the dining room table, centered on my good lace tablecloth, is a very attractive paper turkey Susan made two years ago. On another bookcase in the corner is a globe of the world, and on the buffet is an arrangement of vegetables from the farm. Very good. However, in between all this in full view are the following: Mark's gym bag, slightly wet from yesterday's shower after ball practice; mail waiting for Michael to pick up when he drops by; a basket of dirty laundry that Shirley brought over to do at our house; last Sunday's *Kansas City Star* that never got put in the bag for recycling; two empty coke bottles; Mark's school books; and the baby carrier that little Penny uses while at our house.

I must concede that the interior decorator was probably right. What you can see from the front door does reflect what type of family lives there. Anyone coming into our house can tell right away that they have entered the home of a family of slobs.

TESTING, ONE, TWO, THREE, TESTING

My life as a minister's wife had many periods where I felt I was being tested. Sometimes the one doing the testing was none other than myself. Other times it was someone else.

When I was being Lester's unpaid church secretary, I had a testing experience when we were trying out a new electric typewriter. I usually type fairly well, with a few mistakes and some pauses to look for the right key. But when a typewriter salesman brought a machine for me to try, I felt I was being tested as I typed while he watched. Being an adult, I didn't let things like little tests bother me, so I calmly sat down and typed swiftly: Mos os the rime for all food mrn to vome to the aid fo their ciuntry. Nothing to it! Calm and cool all the way! Since this was an electric typewriter, I asked him where the thingamajig is that returns the top part back to where it should be. After finding the thingamajig, I also found that this typewriter has a helpful key with the letters t and h on the same key. This helpful key is right next to the thingamajig. Under the salesman's watchful eye, I typed several lines quickly and coolly ending eachth linth withth nice Biblical soundth liketh thisth. Since I greatly impressed the salesman with my ability, I passed that test with flying colors.

At home it comes out differently. I was efficiently washing a large pile of sticky dishes and was startled by a voice at my elbow saying, "Why do you do it that way?" It had to be one of the kids. My husband learned long ago this was no way to promote domestic happiness. I replied to my offspring, "Because it is the best way to do it," and efficiently splashed soapsuds into the rinse water and chipped a piece off the plate I was washing.

"Well, it looked like it would be better to rinse the dishes all at once. You have to move them twice this way." In times of tests like these, old maxims are very handy. In this case a virtuous, If a thing's worth doing, it's worth doing well, will usually hush up most kids even if it has nothing to do with the matter at hand. Then it is not necessary for you to think of a real answer.

I passed the second test.

During the years we lived in Butler, I took a couple of night courses at Cottey College to improve my social work skills. As only adults took the course, the teacher trusted us not to cheat. That trust is unnerving in itself. To try to live up to the teacher's trust, I became so aware of my every action that I was afraid to move. First, my nose began to tickle, then run. I reached in my pocket for a Kleenex and suddenly froze. Suppose the teacher thinks I have the answers written on the tissue. I decided to tough it out until the situation had gone beyond casual feigned scratching and rubbings that didn't solve the problem. I had to use a tissue. There was no other way. I decided that if I took it out quickly, blew my nose and returned it to my pocket without glancing at it, the teacher would continue to know of my trustworthiness.

This I did and promptly discovered I had wiped my daughter's bubble gum all over my face. This was the same Kleenex I had used in church right before the children's choir was to sing.

When I completed the test, everyone else seemed to still be busily writing. I couldn't be that much smarter than the rest. I must have missed something. I went back over the entire test, question by question. I was done. I answered everything. But still there were no sounds of others putting away their things. I finally decided I would turn in my paper and leave regardless of the other students. Immediately, when I put on my coat and started to rise, everyone else also moved. The big fakers! Everyone was waiting on someone else.

No, adults don't panic or worry when they are tested. They have maturity and experience to guide them. Oh my, there's a state patrol car behind me. What's my speed? Did I signal at that corner? I sure wish he would pass me.

DRESSING FOR SUCCESS

I recently did some reminiscing about the days when my three oldest were all preschoolers. I remembered how much fun it was to get them and myself all dressed and ready to go at the same time. There was always the problem of which one to get dressed first. If I dressed the baby first and put him safely in a crib or playpen, maybe he wouldn't get dirty before the rest of us got ready. But chances were I'd still have to change him again before I left. Or worse still, if it were early in the morning, he would possibly spit up all over his clothes and need to be completely changed again.

This happened to me the day we were having Shirley baptized at church. I had saved a special dress for the occasion and had her all nicely dressed in her pretty clothes. I then laid her down to go put on my own dress. I came back to find that she had spit up most of her morning bottle all over the dress. We didn't even have running water as this was in the droughts of the fifties and our well had gone dry. Without anything really nice to put on her in place of the special dress, I just mopped it off and hoped nobody noticed. I'm sure the minister must have wondered because the memory lingered on, in odor—even if you couldn't see anything.

However, that was in the days when babies wore bright satin slips with a thin nylon dress, usually white or a soft color, over the slip. The dress had long ribbons attached to each shoulder, so the slipperiness of the baby with the nylon over satin, plus the long ribbons getting tangled around her arms and legs probably distracted the poor minister enough that he didn't notice the smell.

But let's go back to my problems in dressing all of us at once. If I tried to dress the toddler first, there was always a ninety percent chance that he would sit, step, or fall in something before the rest of us were ready. The prize came when I had a toddler dressed ready to go and turned around just in time to see him step into a filled bathtub, shoes, socks, and pants, all instantly dripping wet. I always say it's a good thing children of that age are so cute or we would never survive the toddling years—nor would some of them!

So usually I decided that the best person to dress first was myself. I would leave the shoes and jewelry off until the last minute but get everything else done. Then I would start with the oldest child, then the baby, put the oldest child in charge of watching the baby while I tackled the toddler and put the finishing touches on myself.

I usually followed this procedure to get ready for something important or on Sunday morning to get ready for church. I can tell you that by the time we made it to church, we all really needed our religion. The kids still tell me they can remember those trips into town when I discovered dirt behind their ears, milk on their mouths, or hair unruly. A spit bath in the car was part of our Sunday morning ritual most weeks.

Now that my children are grown and even their children are grown, these things are but a memory. Sunday mornings should be calm and unhurried except that I can't find my glasses that I took off Saturday night as I was doing a crossword puzzle in bed. And Lester's tie clip evidently went on a vacation since last week. And my shoes got pushed so far under the bed that I couldn't reach them without hurting my sore shoulder, and . . .

MARITAL DISCORD

I can't understand why there are more divorces now than there were in the past. The times I have come closest to leaving my husband were when we were doing one of four things, none of which many couples do today.

The four causes of crises in our early married days were these: laying down a new linoleum, putting up or taking down the heating stove, trying to catch or drive cattle or pigs, and, finally, planting a garden.

Many people still plant gardens today, but since we inherited a garden at our third parsonage and became embarrassed as people saw the results of our efforts, we have not planted one ourselves. It is a good thing. There seems to be some law of attraction that causes the straight-line garden planters to marry the helter-skelter type. When we planted a garden, Lester drove stakes, tied a string between them, and planted carefully along the straight line. I, on the other side of the garden, started at one end of the row and planted along as I went. The end result looked like a map of the Mississippi River. But the peas tasted just as good as those grown on the straight lines. We have fewer arguments since we stopped trying to plant a garden.

Driving livestock is also still done by some couples, I am sure, but since we left the farm when Lester went into the ministry, our livestock has consisted of kids, cats, and dogs. Oh yes, we did have a pair of parakeets for several years that would try our patience when we tried to return them to their cages. But our main livestock days are behind us. When we were on the farm, I often was drafted to help corral a stubborn pig or a frightened cow. Invariably, I ended up with the wrong gate closed and the wrong one open as the animals came hurtling by me. I also lost my nerve as I stood as a detour sign for a charging cow and scrambled out of her way instead of diverting her path. Since the livestock was mostly female, I also got my feelings hurt as Lester yelled, "You silly girl, why can't you see what I want you to do?"—only to find that he was talking to the sow or cow and not to me!

But the two main causes for marital discord were linoleum laying and stove placements. Very few people now have the type of stove that you take down each spring, and linoleums are often replaced by inlaid-type tiles or even kitchen carpeting.

Each year we tried to decide when we could safely take down the old stove to allow more room in the house. We never agreed on the time. When we did begin the process, I hovered with a broom, dustpan, and wastebasket, hoping to avoid a mess. It never worked. We always dropped a section of the stovepipe, causing soot to spray over the whole house.

In the fall when we put the stove back up, the same pieces of pipe that fitted nicely in the spring mysteriously shrunk or swelled during the summer to make the fitting very hard or cause the need for some replacement pipes.

Laying linoleum had similar problems. Either the weather was so cold the linoleum cracked or broke as we attempted to unroll it, or it would be so hot that we nearly suffocated trying to fit the pre-measured rug into the pre-measured room. Then we found that somebody goofed and the rug was two inches short on one side and two inches too long on the other. Though it was never anyone's fault, it sure caused a strain as we cut the offending two inches off while crouched in the corner. A slip of the knife and the beautiful linoleum had a split across it that necessitated rearranging the kitchen to hide the tear.

Surely marriages of today have no problems more taxing that these four. So I still can't see what could cause the higher divorce rate today.

MACHINES AND ME

I think that machines in my life have taken a dislike to me and purposely are causing me trouble. This machine age is great, but when the machines start becoming full of petty dislikes against me, then that's too much.

For example: I used to go out to get in the car to start it and had to work for several minutes before the Chevy started properly. My son would come out, do the exact things that I did, and the engine purred smoothly on the first touch on the accelerator. If I get stalled in the car and have to summon help, as soon as the garage man arrives, the car is happy to run again. It refuses to show any of its problems to the mechanic.

In the house the same thing happens. I have trouble with the toaster keeping the bread down long enough for the toast to become brown. I call Lester and he pushes the lever down. The bread browns nicely and pops up just right for the butter. The garbage disposal will fail to work until I summon help and then miraculously it is spinning garbage into shreds as it is intended to do.

The telephone can be very full of static or will not ring at all until the repairman comes. Then it will sound clear as a bell.

But the worst case of machinitis I have ever had was in connection with a copying machine in the welfare office in Butler where I worked for three years. Everyone in the office could walk up to the machine, insert three sheets of paper, push a button, wait a minute, and have a bright clear copy of their original. I walked up to the machine, inserted three sheets of paper, pushed the button, waited a minute, and had a completely black sheet of paper come out. Other times it would just be dark brown, or half brown and half black. I did not change any settings and used the same materials. I secretly practiced at lunch time to find out what was going wrong, and sometimes, then, the copies came out clear. When I got back to work, however, and needed a copy in a hurry, all I would get would be pitch dark blackness.

Naturally, this is embarrassing. To be the only one who can't operate a simple machine is downright humiliating. So I faked it. After inserting my papers, I'd look approvingly at my black copy, walk back to my desk as if satisfied and file away my coal black piece of paper.

This, of course, causes trouble because no one needs a file of black paper with no legible words on them. So I would pretend an emergency, or a conference, and then ask one of the girls up front if she could make copies for me while I rushed off on an imaginary errand.

I don't think I fooled anyone, but I did get better copies this way, plus a lot of exercise dashing around in my emergencies.

There are some people who are not intended to live in the machine age. I think I am one of them, one of them, one of them. Oh oh, I think I must have hit the repeat button by mistake.

HIGHWAYS TO ????

The present generation spends a great portion of time in a car—driving for pleasure, family errands, or business. Since there is so much attention given to the automobile industry, I felt there needed to be changes made in some of the songs and theology about the hereafter. Very few of us are really concerned about golden slippers or sweet chariots. But mention a bright red sports car and we take notice.

Therefore, I have found some explanations of what I feel either Heaven or Hell could be like in our motorized age. Let's start on the good side. Let's go to Heaven in a motorcar.

The first thing you will find in the highway of the hereafter will be a four-lane divided pavement that has all the charm and scenic views of a one-lane blacktop road. There will be a few distant cars enjoying the breathtaking scenery. Of course, there will be no signs to mar the beauty, except when you want to know something. Then a sign will miraculously appear to direct you to the right spot. There will be exit ramps every time you need them, and they will go in the direction you expect. They won't send you north to go east or south to go west.

The car you will be driving will require very little attention from you and will keep the perfect temperature for each occupant of the car. The sun will be shining (whoever heard of a cloudy Heaven?) but there will be just a hint of haze over the sun to keep it from glaring in your eyes.

Your car will be full of loved ones, but they will all be happy and singing—the same song even. No one will need to go to the restroom. No one will be hungry or thirsty. Everyone will be delighted with his or her place in the car. Those in the middle will enjoy sitting in the middle.

But suppose you've not lived the good life. Perhaps you will be spending eternity driving the road from Harrisonville to Holden (or any narrow, rolling blacktop road) on a foggy night, with a weak headlight, a gas tank that shows nearly E, and one tire you're not too sure of.

If this is not terrifying enough, perhaps you may endlessly drive down an eight-lane divided highway at 70 MPH with traffic thick on all sides. The exit you need leaves from the right while you are in the extreme left lane. Two children in the back seat have announced that they need to go to the restroom, and one says she is going to vomit now. Your spouse is telling you that if you had listened to him/her at that last turn you would be in the right lane and could get out at the next exit easily. The radio is loudly playing a song you hate, and the bus in front of you is emitting diesel fuel that you are sucking into your blower.

Perhaps more examples are still needed? Here's one to make a real believer out of you. You are driving a car with a standard shift for the first time in ten years. You are caught in the middle of an intersection in downtown Kansas City and can't get the car in the correct gear. The lights have changed twice and cars are honking at you from four sides. Some nice Biblical words are being used in an unbiblical way by a big burly man who gets out of his car to come toward you.

I don't know if it's a reflection of my character or my driving ability, but I've never experienced my description of Heaven. But I believe my car and I have been in the other place many times!

THE IMPERFECTIONS OF BEING PERFECT

I have been trying hard not to be perfect. You see, I feel that people really don't care too much for the perfect person. They feel more at home with someone who is a bit of a slob. So I am trying hard to establish a reputation that I fill people's needs by being less than perfect in every respect.

For example, how many people do you know who are dearly beloved because they have a spotless house? We may grudgingly say, "She's an immaculate housekeeper." But oh, we enjoy it when we catch her with her tables dusty or papers all over the floor. Then we can feel she is really one of us. I try to make my friends happy by letting them feel superior to me. When they come to my home, they don't start making comparisons with their own stained floors and cobwebby ceilings. When we were living in parsonages and visitors came and saw gym shoes on the piano and the cat asleep on the clean laundry, they said, "The poor child needs my friendship. She doesn't really know how to run her house." So they came over often and felt comfortable because they looked so good compared to me as a housekeeper.

Then there's the matter of dressing well. We all like to look our best in the eyes of others. But people that look too good find that others aren't very happy about it because they suddenly feel that they have ten thumbs and three legs when they stand next to someone who looks like she has just stepped out of a bandbox. No one objects to standing next to me because of my perfections. They feel very well-groomed and at ease.

My flowers never quite make it to their potential. But we have lovely bouquets given to us by friends who notice that my posies are on the sickly side. When we used to have a vegetable garden, we always ate best on the years our garden didn't do well. Friends noticed and showered us with their evidences of green thumbitis. And at the church basket dinners after people saw my casseroles and pies, they ended up sending all sorts of goodies home with us to feed the poor pastor and the kiddies that had to eat my cooking all the time.

So you can see how happy I have made people all my life by trying hard not to be a perfect person. In fact, I have done such a good job of being imperfect that I even have Lester fooled. When he read this essay he said, "I can tell everyone that you have reached your goal."

It's nice to do one thing really well. I do a great job of being imperfect.

WAITRESS WOES

Nothing makes you appreciate another person more than having to do the same type of work for a few hours. For years I had not thought too much about the problems waitresses must have. But in several of our churches I have had the job of waiting tables at fund-raising dinners. I now see that it is not an easy job to do.

As I worked I kept muttering, "Serve from the right and take from the left." Or is it the other way around? I never really knew. Some people are very helpful and hand things to the waitress and move to allow her room to place the plates properly. On the other hand, others will sit with both elbows protruding until she has to practically lie on their backs to reach the table in front of them. At times like this you begin to remember the commercials for Dial and Right Guard and wonder how this close contact is coming across to the diners.

Somehow or other the table I wait on is always the one that is longer—with guests who eat faster and eat more than any of the others at the banquet. It's a funny thing though—every other lady waiting tables says the same thing about her table.

Actually serving the food isn't so bad. The guests are usually hungry and still sitting approximately as we arranged the chairs and plates, and the table is still nice and neat.

By the time it comes to serve the dessert course, folks have begun to shift their chairs. They have conversations down the table, over their backs, and have shifted their chairs to hear their friends more clearly. They also have moved their dishes and generally made it very hard to move up and down the aisles with a filled tray of cake.

Clearing the table is something else. Many will push their dirty dishes away from them to allow room for looking at their programs or resting their arms. Therefore, in a crowded aisle, we have to balance a tray in one hand, and with the other, reach over a broad shoulder to the middle of the table while poised on one foot. It's something equal to an Olympic gymnast's performance. I often think churches could raise even more money by selling tickets just to watch us at work. We must be a comical sight in our contortions.

However, I have a gimmick. Being a little older than the others who usually wait tables, I grab some young girl who is helping for the first time and say, "It's awfully hard to hold a tray and clear at the same time. Why don't we work together and I'll hold your tray for you." This seems a generous offer, but actually then all I have to do is walk and hold the tray while she does the reaching, the squirming, and arranging the dishes on my tray. I just trudge along like an old plodding mule and wait for my load to get heavy. I'm afraid some girls are getting on to me though, and one of these days someone will make me that same generous offer to carry my tray. I'll have to be working on a comeback for that just in case.

DUSTY MEMORIES

Today I received one of those cute forwarded messages on the Internet. It was entitled "Dust If You Must." The premise of the essay was that there are more important things to do in life than to keep your house clean. It ended with the promise that when you died, you yourself will make more dust. I certainly agree with these thoughts. But it wasn't always that easy to ignore dust when we lived in parsonages.

I always tried to keep the front room, or the room that was visible from the front door, as neat as was possible with four children and various dog or cat pets in the house. That doesn't count the aquarium for tropical fish that usually sported handprints all over the sides or the cage for Martha and George, the parakeets that were bought on February 22. The cage was neat, but the area around it was usually sprinkled with birdseed.

Our first parsonage was quite small, and all these necessities for our children, who had just been removed from the farm, needed to be in the front room. To make matters worse, the front room had a large picture window on the front that faced the busiest street in the little town. I would sometimes deliberately take a drive past the house to see what I could see from the road. It wasn't too much comfort, because I could see not only the living room, but I could see through the living room to the six cereal boxes stacked on top of the refrigerator in the kitchen. Each family member preferred a different kind of cereal and since there were some unwanted animals in the house in addition to our pets, the top of the refrigerator was the safest place to keep our variety of breakfast foods.

One solution was to keep the drapes closed, but I do not believe in living in a house without sunlight. Besides, I wanted to see who was driving by as much as they wanted to see what we were doing inside our house.

A few years later, in a larger parsonage, I devised the system of having the vacuum cleaner sitting in the living room as an indication that I was just getting ready to clean when the visitor stopped by. I hadn't learned this ploy at this time, however, so I waged a losing battle against the dirt and clutter our lively household created.

One of our strongest supporters in the church had the habit of stopping to look in the picture window as she walked from her car across the sidewalk that went right by the window. She would literally stop and put her hands on either side of her face to block out reflections from the street as she looked in the window. One time she mentioned that she didn't want to interrupt us if we were in prayer! There was very little chance for that!

But back to the dust. When I had some of the community children meet in the parsonage for their 4-H meetings (I still hadn't left all of the farm behind) and became a Cub Scout den mother also meeting in the home, I soon found that people were more impressed with what I did than with what I didn't do.

I still worried about the mess, but I learned to explain it to folks that visited by asking their advice on some project that was obviously being carried out in the room.

Now, in retirement, I live back in the country. I am some distance from a country road. My main visitors are family members and our three cats. I can write "I love you" in the dust on almost any piece of furniture in the house. And if any of my friends did stop by, we would have too much to talk about to notice my dusty house. We might even talk about the new minister who is coming to our church and wonder if those family members will be good housekeepers.

3

HEY, I THINK I'M CATCHING ON

Practice makes perfect, the maxim says,
So I practiced every day
Till now I've reached perfection
If you can look at things my way.

CUES FROM THE PEWS

I have often wondered how the spouses of actors feel when their loved ones are performing. I doubt that many of them attend every performance and sit in the audience of a live play every night and matinee during the run. Most spouses of ministers, however, are there every Sunday—and sometimes for more than one service. We see and hear almost every *performance* of our loved one.

Early in Lester's ministry I not only heard his sermons every week, but I also typed them for him the night before. With this background, it is very easy to notice a mistake or to see where a point was weakened because of an ad-lib that didn't add to the message. When the minister is on a circuit (where he is going to more than one church in the same morning), the wife has often been known to use the time while driving between the churches for a sermon critique. This is probably no help at all to the minister who must then realize at certain points in his talk that he should change his wording. The new words, hastily inserted, may not fit as well as the first draft.

After Lester had officially retired, he did several part-time interim ministries. One of these had three services each Sunday morning. One was at nine, one at ten, and the last at eleven-fifteen. There was a total of about thirty miles of driving between the churches, so in addition to catching his breath and gearing for the next place, he also had to drive narrow county roads quite fast to make the schedule.

I rode with him on most Sundays, and by the time I was hearing the sermon for the third time, I sometimes gasped and thought he was repeating himself. He was—from the last church. Somehow I could never enter into the service as a worshiper, but I was always feeling that I had to micromanage everything, even if I never mentioned to Lester what I noticed. After all, being on your feet speaking during three services is enough of an ordeal for a retired man without having his wife make suggestions when it was too late to do anything about it.

The members of an earlier church had great fun teasing me about my actions one special Sunday. I knew the choir had gone to a lot of trouble and had practiced hard for an anthem they were to sing. There were other special things going on during the service also which made the order of service slightly different.

When it was time for the anthem, Lester went ahead with the prayer before the sermon. The choir members all looked at each other in surprise, but since they sat behind the pulpit, Lester couldn't see them. I could. I quickly grabbed the bulletin and with my pen wrote in large letters the word, "CHOIR". I held it up at chest level from my seat about a third of the way back and waved it slightly as he ended the prayer. He didn't notice it. As he started into the sermon, I lifted the sign higher and by now the members of the choir had seen it and were smiling at one another. However, Lester was intent on his message and didn't notice either me or the slight activity in the choir loft.

I pulled the sign down into my lap until the sermon was over, but then I immediately put it up even higher as preparations for the offertory were beginning. Since most of the people sitting near me had noticed my activity, Lester finally saw that everyone was looking at me. Then he saw the sign. Without showing any concern or embarrassment he calmly said, "I see a signal that the choir is now ready to honor us with their anthem." After the laughter died down, we enjoyed a wonderful message in song. I am not sure how many of us heard the spoken message that had preceded it. But I think many people remembered the stage wife who felt she had to butt in.

FUNERAL MISHAPS

Funerals are often a mixture of tears and laughter. The family that has come together to honor their departed loved one will often share humorous stories about their loved one as well as making the sad preparations for life with one missing. Ministers and funeral home personnel feel privileged to be part of that process of celebration and healing. But they also have behind the scene stories that they enjoy sharing after the service has finished.

In my own middle age plus years, two family funerals have had humorous twists. Following my brother Ralph's service in his church, the family was lining up in cars to go to the cemetery. Ralph's four children rode in the family car provided by the funeral home. His in-laws and grandchildren were in a family van, which had been parked by the entrance of the church. I was in my nephew's car with Ralph's other siblings and other cars were also following. When the hearse and family car pulled out, John, who was driving the van, was caught off guard but hurried to get behind the wheel and followed the procession out the church driveway.

After a few blocks, my sister Ellen and I began to think this was a roundabout way to reach the cemetery, which we had been shown on an earlier trip to visit Ralph. We decided that the funeral director was avoiding the traffic routes. However, very soon we realized that the car that John was following was not going to the cemetery at all but had returned to the retirement village where Ralph had been living.

In a panic, John ran back to our car to confess he didn't even know where the cemetery was located. We were able to tell him and our segment of the processional, which included six or seven cars, turned around and finally arrived at the grave site where Ralph's anxious children were wondering what on earth had happened to the rest of their families. We all thought Ralph would have laughed with us over this experience.

At my sister Kathryn's service, we delayed the beginning of the service because we knew that a van full of her special friends from her retirement apartment complex were on the way to the funeral, which was in another town in Connecticut. Through cell phone calls we found that they were on their way but had become lost. Since these friends were in their eighties and nineties, Kathryn's children didn't want to start without them. The organ played . . . and played . . . and played until at last the ladies began coming in the back of the church. However, since these were older women and the trip had taken much longer than they expected, they each needed to use the restroom rather urgently when they arrived. Therefore, they came up the side aisle of the church and headed straight through to the restrooms just beyond the sanctuary. After they returned by twos (it was a two-holer), the poor organist could finally quit playing and the beautiful service began. Again, we agreed that Kathryn would have smiled and appreciated her friends' situation.

Another incident happened at a graveside service Lester was conducting. Not having attended this service, I heard Lester's own version of what happened.

He followed the casket bearers to the grave site and was preparing to position himself at the head of the casket. The funeral home had spread artificial grass over the raw and muddy dirt around the grave. Lester stepped to his position and instantly realized that the grass had covered part of the grave opening. One of his legs went completely in the grave as he suddenly sat on the edge of the hole. He sprang up immediately before the family arrived and conducted the ceremony with one very damp and dirty pant leg. The funeral home operator had seen what had happened and later said he was afraid Lester was going to go completely down. Lester returned home telling me that he now had one foot in the grave.

MORE FUNERAL MISHAPS

I just couldn't get all of the stories about things that happen at funerals in one essay. Not all of these stories happened to us, but they were shared by other friends who did experience or witness them.

In a neighboring town there was a funeral home director who had the reputation of drinking rather heavily. At one service on a rainy day, this man was preparing to protect the widow from the rain as she emerged from the church door. He had one of these large black umbrellas that two people can walk under comfortably. At the top of the umbrella is a spike that allows it to double as a cane and it keeps the fabric from rubbing on the ground as it is carried. When the woman left the church, the funeral home director, with a flourish, spread open the umbrella over her head. She gasped and reached for her hair. The woman had been wearing a wig, with her hair in pin curls under the wig. As he opened the umbrella, the director spiked her wig. It rested on top of the large umbrella while the poor widow stood there with her pin curls shining.

The wife of another funeral home director tells a story about one of the early funerals she assisted with. It was nearly time for the service to begin and she didn't know where her husband was. She then heard the words, "Pssst, Mary, come here." She located the voice coming from behind a door and found him standing there in wet pants, shoes, and socks. He told her to rush home and get him some dry shoes and another suit in a hurry. In making preparations for the flowers and arrangements in an unfamiliar church building, he had opened the door of what he thought was a closet. While feeling for the light switch, he stepped off into the baptistry! Mary got him his clothes in a hurry and none of the family was aware that their church almost had a newly baptized convert.

My last story on this subject is not humorous. On a snowy winter day, Lester and a visiting minister were conducting a service in a rather large church. I had arrived early when Lester needed to be there and sat in the sanctuary waiting for time for the service. In midwest towns, some people tend to arrive early for funerals so I expected some of my friends to come fairly soon. No one came to join me. Then I realized it was time for the service. The two ministers, an organist, and soloist were in the chancel area, but I was the only one out in the pews. As the family was about to arrive, the funeral home personnel saw the situation and sent all of the employees in to sit in various parts of the sanctuary so it wouldn't look completely empty.

I had not wanted to come to the service because of the weather and schedule, but if I hadn't, absolutely no one would have been there except those conducting the service. That was one time I was glad my conscience caused me to do my duty as a minister's wife.

THE MINISTER'S FAMILY CAT

(Maxi was a very special cat in our family in the 1970s. He was born in the basement of one parsonage and lived in two others as our family grew smaller when the older kids left. He died under our bed in a fourth parsonage.)

I like being who I am, but at times I imagine what it would be like if I were to change places for one day with another person. I recently began thinking how it would be to have spent a day as Maxi. (So named because he wore a floor-length fur coat. Unfortunately, his litter mate, Mini, did not reach adulthood but died of complications of her spaying operation.)

The day I trade places with Maxi, I will walk slowly into the living room where my loved ones are sitting. Instead of the usual, "Hey, Mom, will you help me with this?" or "Don't stand there, you're blocking the TV," I will be called by each person in the room. "Come sit with me, come on, come here, that's right. See, he does like me best! Nice kitty. Oh, do you want this chair? O.K. I will sit on the floor. Did you see that? Wasn't that cute? He wants the best chair."

As Maxi, when I get good and rested in the best chair, I will slowly rise and walk toward the kitchen. If no one moves, I will come back into the living room just slightly and make a small pitiful "Mew." That's all it will take and I will instantly be offered several delicacies from the refrigerator. Just for fun I may pretend I do not like the first thing offered me. It won't matter. They'll keep looking until they find something suitable. I will eat all I want of exactly what I want. No one will suggest I should fix the family something to eat. No one will expect me to clean up afterwards.

Since I have rested well and eaten well, I may now choose to spend some time in a leisurely beauty treatment. I will not be told to hurry up for heaven's sake. There will be no suggestion that my dress is too short, too long, too tight, or the wrong color. No, everyone will gather round and admire how beautiful I look. "Have you ever seen a prettier cat? Look at how his fur glistens! You pretty, pretty kitty!" Much love, petting, and stroking will accompany all this.

Sometimes a person likes to be alone, so I will coolly leave all my admiring public and find a secluded place to rest some more. They won't say, "What's the matter with you? How come you're in here all alone?" They won't bang on the door and demand to be let in. Everyone will naturally realize that I just want to be alone at times. They will remind each other that I am tired of them now and will leave me alone.

A nap on the softest bed, maybe on top of the pillows, will be a good place for my time alone. I will prefer to have a spot where the sun shines in and very little noise can reach me. It won't matter if I mess up the bedspread a little bit. No one will expect me to remake the bed or clean any paw prints I might leave.

A little excitement may be needed soon, so I will go to the front door and again utter the one small word, "Mew." The door will instantly open. I may choose to stand in the doorway for a few minutes admiring the view before I decide to stroll outside. It doesn't matter. The door will be open until I make up my mind. (However, I will not push that too far as the man of the house does not take too kindly to open doors in the winter!)

Outside I will do whatever I want to do for as long as I feel like doing it, knowing that as soon as I wish to return inside, I will be welcomed eagerly.

When I do return, I will not be asked where I was for so long or what did I bring them. Everyone will be delighted to have me back just because I am me.

The day I am Maxi, no one will ask me to do anything but exist. The day I am Maxi, everyone I care about will love me and approve of everything I do, asking nothing in return. The day I am Maxi, I will be beautiful, rested, well-fed, and content.

But the day I am Maxi, I can only say one word, and one day is about all I can stand of that. I think I'm more content being Carolyn and able to talk, even if I am not beautiful, rested, and well-fed.

LIGHTING ONE LITTLE CANDLE

Back in the 1970s during the power shortage emergency, the mayor of our town, Butler, Missouri, made the suggestion that if each family would dine by candlelight, they would save enough electricity to light their Christmas tree for an hour or so each night. Our family responded wholeheartedly. We always enjoyed an occasional candlelight meal. And we also liked to have the living room lighted only by candles and tree lights during the Christmas season. (This was before we found out that the reason Lester always came down with a bad cold during the Christmas season was because he was allergic to the smoke of candles. Following the Christmas Eve candlelight ceremonies in our churches, I would have to put out the candles to help him avoid the smoke.)

There is something about candlelight that brings out the best in everyone. For example, our manners improved greatly at the table when we dined by candlelight. Each member of the family received at least one scorched wrist from the boarding-house reach over the candle before we learned that it is more comfortable to ask for food to be passed than to singe the hair on our arms while reaching for food.

Likewise at the table when the lighting is dim, more attention was given to the food and drink and therefore there were fewer spills. When you have to look closely to see if it is the hamburger or the bread and jelly you are pouring ketchup on, you tend to spill less ketchup. Also we didn't leave the gallon jug of milk on the table to allow for second helpings, because with a single candle at the center of the table, something as large as a gallon jug of milk can eclipse a whole side of the table.

Loud talk was avoided because it started the flame fluttering and those of us with motion sickness couldn't take that. So we found our candlelight meals were accompanied by nice soft conversation, passing food, turning of the head to cough or sneeze, and less spills and messes. Of course, when the meal was over and the lights were turned back on, we found that maybe there were more spills than we realized. But in the darkness, who could tell?

I love to entertain by candlelight. In the dim, romantic light of a few well-placed candles, no one can spot a smudge in the dust, a scratch on the furniture, a patch in the upholstery, or even cobwebs on the ceiling. If there is a part of the room that is less attractive, the candles can be placed to throw that area into darkness and highlight the more attractive spots. Also when it is fairly dark in the room, a middle-aged woman can look very alluring and young. The wrinkles, gray hairs, and sags don't show in the candle glow, and even the men can look like Cary Grant instead of Columbo. Of course, you need to avoid standing directly in front of a candle because the shadow you throw can be enormous which will destroy the allusion of grace and add instead a dimension of elephantitis.

We felt that we saved enough electricity with the candles to light the tree for a while each night while we were watching television or visiting in the living room. Actually we probably used less light than if we had used the usual reading lamps.

Since Christmas is designated as the time of the coming of light, our experiences in the candlelight that year made us appreciate the light even more.

I tried to remember that the next morning when I was cleaning off a pile of candle wax from my favorite table.

BASKET DINNERS

I have gone to many basket dinners in my life. These and potluck suppers are favorites in most of the churches Lester served. This invention of someone must have started back in the caveman days when some man got tired of his wife's brontosaurus burgers and wanted a variety. Today it can be fun and exciting to get out and eat other people's cooking . . . if you didn't have to take something yourself.

My problem is choosing what to take. I seem to end up with one dish that should be served piping hot and one that should remain chilled. Getting the two dishes, plus the large sack of potato chips that always makes an easy third dish to the meal without having lukewarm dishes, involves careful packaging and planning.

When I had over-eager helpers to carry the basket to the car, that often caused disaster as the baked beans spilled into the Jell-O on the way to the car. No one in our family seems to realize that car seats slant to the back and that a basket with liquid dishes in it will spill if it is set on the back seat.

Some things mix well, but if they do, I prefer to mix them myself, on purpose, and not have them mixed on the way to the church.

A rule of thumb for basket dinners used to be to take one dish for each member of your family that will be eating. This was a mammoth undertaking when all four children were at home. Now that our family has shrunk, I sometimes feel guilty just taking two or three dishes. This is especially true when one dish is cottage cheese and another is the aforementioned potato chips.

When I was a bride, I took a pie to a basket dinner at the school where Lester was teaching. Although every other dish was nearly empty, my pie was completely intact. One slice had been cut but had not been removed from the dish. I had to go retrieve the pie after the dinner and take it home. I never did see what was so wrong with that pie. To this day if I see an untouched dish at a basket dinner, I will take some of it, even if I have to leave it uneaten on my plate. I remember too well the tears I shed over my own uneaten pie.

Another problem with covered dish dinners is you usually end up sitting next to the person who brought the dish that you can't stand to eat. There you sit with a mound of gunk on your plate that tastes awful, and the person next to you mentions how that was her mother's favorite recipe. But that is better than if your neighbor doesn't mention anything about the dish being hers and you ask her if she has tasted that awful stuff!

When the meal is over and you are picking up your dishes, someone will always offer her leftovers for the minister's family to take home. Sometimes I think she just doesn't want to bother with putting the one slice of pie in with her potato salad and green beans. By the time we get home, again with the basket sitting on the slanting back seat, we have onions in the melted Jell-O, cake in the mashed potatoes and the chicken bones brought home for the cats—all mixed in with the good meatloaf.

One look and we decide the whole mess cannot be saved.

Our dogs and cats loved for us to go to basket dinners. I'm not sure that I really liked them all that well.

RESPONSIBILITIES

(This essay was written when we lived in Butler in the 1970s.)

When you get possessions, you also get responsibilities. We used to be carefree stay-at-homers who sat comfortably in our cool home and watched others frantically pack up and leave each weekend, supposedly to relax. We didn't have to pack, arrange for the dog's care, cook extra food, and travel for miles.

No, we just kicked off our shoes, put up the hammock, and sent the kids off to the pool. We could even know that we didn't have to hurry to return home in time for church on Sunday or get a substitute to take over our responsibilities.

But no more. We have acquired a possession. So now we have a responsibility. You see, we bought a foldout tent trailer for our recent vacation. But we can't stop there. Once we have this nice trailer sitting in our driveway, we have responsibilities. We can't just fold it up and leave it alone for a year. No, since we have this thing, we have to use it or feel awfully extravagant for having bought it in the first place.

Okay, since we're going to have to use it, it seems odd to use it in our own driveway. (However, the kids have enjoyed their campouts at home in it.) No, we need to go somewhere.

So now we get ready for a two-day campout. It has taken most of our off-work hours the day before we leave to get all our gear ready to go, shop for the food, wash the clothes we need, and find a place to put it all in the trailer.

The day we leave it takes two or three false starts before we remember everything we need and actually get going.(I'll never forget the two-week trip when I forgot to take any extra, rather necessary undergarments and had to wash my one set in the showers whenever I could and either wear them wet or do without until they dried.)

But we finally get going and drive to a beautiful spot on the lake. There we set up our trailer, sweep it out, fix the supper, wash the dishes, and finally unfold our lawn chairs and sit down to relax while the kids run to the lake to swim.

The big difference between here and home is that at home our bath is ten feet away and the neighbors are a hundred feet away. Here our neighbor is only ten feet away and the restrooms are a quarter mile away.

So why are we here? Well, we're relaxing and having fun. It must be fun. There are a hundred other people sharing our campground. They seem to be having lots of fun as they laugh and talk past midnight each night. And the people on the other side seem to be having fun as they get up before dawn to go fishing. They call back and forth to each other as they get started—to show how much fun they are having.

We just didn't know what we were missing all those years we just stayed home to relax. But now we don't miss out. Now we have a possession and we are using it. We're going to enjoy it even if it kills us.

FEELING DOWN IN THE MOUTH?

Have you been to a dentist lately? The new conveniences and furniture make the whole experience a joy—for the dentist. He can sit in comfort and look easily into your gaping mouth as you lie supported on your neck in a padded medieval torture chair. It gives you a glorious rosy complexion as all the blood runs to your head. You have ample time to observe your feet near the ceiling and may contemplate the beauty of your scuffed loafers for fifteen minutes while your lips get tingly, then numb.

I always wonder why dentists have beautiful drapes, a nice view from the window, and attractively painted walls. All you see from the moment you sit down is the aforementioned feet, the clock on the wall, a large square of bright lights, and numerous gleaming appliances which tend to get you nicely uptight in a very few moments.

An interlude happens when the dentist comes in cheerily, asks a pleasant question, then just as you begin to answer, immediately puts both his hands, his assistant's hand with a sump pump attached, and three picks and shovels in your mouth. Thoughtfully, the pretty assistant (they are always pretty) places a towel across your eyes so you can't see the execution. This towel seems to make your whole plump body instantly become invisible to the dentist and his helpers. They become engaged in lively conversations with each other as they blast, probe, poke, and siphon in your mouth. Your stiffened body might indicate death, but your mind and ears are acutely aware of the conversation. When the towel slips slightly and you are staring up into the dentist's nostrils three inches above your eyeballs, you are quite sure you do exist.

After the dentist speedily finishes his work, you discover morsels of filling have lodged just east of your tonsils and try to make your friends aware of this. Finally, they apply the suction to the proper spot—and apply—and apply—and apply. As you rapidly become dehydrated, you fear to move your tongue or swallow lest you will completely disappear into the intruding suction tube.

In the olden days, at this point you would be offered a dainty paper cup of water to swish. But the new method leaves you still on your head while your entire mouth is quietly swabbed with a sticky, sweetish goob called fluoride. When you gag on this, the assistant helpfully hands you half a box of Kleenex and tells you not to swallow, drink, or eat for thirty minutes. This leaves only one rather indelicate alternative.

You leave the inner sanctum to enter the lobby, being very conscious that your stiffened lip cannot detect the dripping fluoride and that you probably look like a mad dog. Invariably you will see a former acquaintance, possibly from your last church, who would love to talk a moment, but you want nothing more than a hole to crawl in while you return to normal.

Only one goodie remains—the bill. As I receive it, I

vow that the only way I'll get even is to have one of my grandchildren become a dentist and support me in my toothless old age.

PICTURE THIS

I may have developed a condition called flash-bulbitis. It seems that wherever I go, I come away annoyed at the number of people who ruin an event because of their photography craze.

I recently attended a child's birthday party where the main item of business was to take pictures of every smile, every move, and every mouthful eaten by the birthday child. Before long the young guests were either hamming it up for the camera or in tears.

My dislike of this custom began when my parents were celebrating their golden anniversary. Our two-year-old son became so terrified of the constant flashing around him that he cried through the whole two-day celebration. My memories of the affair are very moist ones, filled with tears, hiccoughs, and sobs. We have good pictures of all the beautiful people there, dressing for the event, greeting others at the door, cutting the cake, drinking the punch, but only two that included our young pride and joy. One is of him in an exhausted sleep on an aunt's lap, and the other was his being held screaming in a picture of all the grandchildren.

As the years went on, this child and our others grew up, but I constantly had my enjoyment of big events in their lives marred by others' insistence on picture taking. When Shirley received her high school diploma, I literally could not see her, as the parent in front of me stood up to get a good shot of his offspring who was getting ready to go across the stage. I posed many a proud shot at home before and after the ceremony, but I hope that didn't bother anyone else, except maybe her date for the evening who had to wait a while for this posing.

When we are on vacations, we often see someone rush madly up to a breathtaking view, snap a picture and rush off. One gets the feeling I've heard expressed often that people don't know if they've enjoyed their vacations until they come home and develop their films—unless they have a digital camera that can tell them right away that they're having a good time.

Lester always told the families of the bride and groom at weddings he performed not to take any pictures that use a flash after the procession down the aisle was finished. That didn't keep others from snapping away, however. At one wedding the professional photographer positioned himself right in the aisle and walked backward in a crouching position as the bride came down the aisle. What made it even more jarring for this elegant wedding was the fact that he was wearing blue jeans and a tee shirt. I'm sure the pictures looked good from that close-up position, but at the ceremony itself all eyes were on the gyrations of the photographer and not on the bride.

I think the prize of photographic foolishness has to come to me, however. When Michael was graduating from basic training in the army, we went to the ceremony. As the soldiers were marching in formation we found his unit and spotted him. I took a whole roll of film of him, marching out on that field. When it was over, we tried to find him and discovered that he had drawn KP duty that morning and wasn't even in the ceremony.

We have a lot of good pictures of someone's son, however.

LESSONS IN GRACIOUSNESS

One of the privileges we experienced during the years of Lester's ministry was to be the minister and wife to a small African-American congregation, called Mt. Zion United Methodist Church. This small brick church stood across the street from a frame church of the African Methodist Episcopal denomination. The African-American community in Butler was small, probably around 150 persons.

Lester was a resident minister to the Ohio Street United Methodist Church, preaching at Mt. Zion just two times a month. An out-of-town minister who came the other two Sundays each month served the other church. Therefore, Lester was often called on to minister to members of both congregations since he was right there in town. Many members of each church attended the services of the other denomination as well as their own, so the attendance was often twice the number of enrolled members. That is an unusual experience for a minister.

Most of the youth were in the Mt. Zion Church and our teen-aged children had several friends in that church. In fact, we often had the two youth groups meeting together in the basement of our parsonage.

The United Methodist Women included the Mt. Zion women as a circle in their unit, and I had the privilege of being a part of that circle. I became very aware of the way the white people, while trying to be inclusive, continued to put up barriers to complete desegregation. One example was at a meeting of the women from both churches. A well-meaning member of the Ohio Street Church gave a history of the integration process in the town. She used the terms "we" and "they" continually throughout the talk, and she often used phrases like, "We were very happy to have them in our school." None of the Mt. Zion members showed any resentment during the meeting and were very cordial throughout the refreshment period afterward. Later at their circle meeting I mentioned my embarrassment at the incident, and they acknowledged they had felt the slight but realized it was not intended to be hurtful.

When our son was playing varsity basketball on the school team, one of his buddies was a Mt. Zion youth whose grandmother tried to attend every one of his games, as did Lester and I. Often Lester would be coming from an out-of-town meeting and we would meet at the game. Sometimes I asked for a ride from the group from Mt. Zion to avoid taking so many cars. One time Lester was coming to an important game from a meeting and the grandmother and I were driving from Butler on a snowy night. When we got there, the gymnasium was packed. Lester had arrived earlier and was trying to save seats for Helen and me. As we walked through the gymnasium lobby, Helen slipped slightly because of snow on her shoes. I reached out to steady her with my arm around her. We stood in the doorway looking for Lester or for an empty spot in the bleachers when I realized that everyone was looking at the door. I turned behind me to see what was going on. Then I realized that what they were looking at was us. This segregated town was not used to seeing two women of different races standing arm in arm with each other.

Lester caught our attention and signaled for us to come to his seat. He had not been able to save a seat but was going to give us his. When we climbed to his location, there suddenly was plenty of room as people moved away from us as if we had the plague.

Throughout this experience, Helen remained as poised and sweet as ever, showing no sign of anger or fear. Afterward she confessed to me that she was a little afraid but had learned much earlier not to let fear keep her from going ahead with her life.

Racial slurs were directed at her grandson who was one of the very good players on our team, but she showed no sign that she heard them. Our son, who was actually playing in the game, heard them easily, as did his friend. They kept their cool; we won the game and got home safely.

This happened in the early 1970s. Let's hope things are different today.

DREAM ALONG WITH ME

Shakespeare mentions he might "sleep, perchance to dream." I'm not sure that is always desirable. Some of my dreams are no comfort to me at all, and I would just as soon they would stay away. Psychologists tell us that dreams are what keep us sane. If we are kept from dreaming by being awakened just when we begin to dream, over a long period of time, we might have real wide-awake problems to deal with. That may be, but some of my asleep problems give me troubles too.

I have come up with a gimmick to give myself some sleepy time comfort. I am in the midst of a terrible dream, usually about some member of my family, and I am so unhappy or so terrified that I am ready to cry out or scream. But, while still in my dreams, I tell myself, "Don't worry. This is just a dream. It's not real," and then I go on with the dream but become less upset about it. I don't know how I developed this skill, or if it is unusual, but I'm sure glad I finally learned to do this.

In our family we have big discussions about whether we dream in color or in black and white. It seems odd to even wonder, since most of us are privileged to see life in color, why wouldn't we dream in color? However, some of the family members insist that their dreams are in black and white. With my vividly colored dreams, I smugly feel as superior as an owner of a color TV set versus a mere black and white.

I have had one dream regularly ever since I was ready to leave elementary school. I am always walking up a steep hill to a school. Sometimes it is the big junior high I attended. Other times it is the Woodrow Wilson Senior High School or a building on a college campus. I am late and I can't seem to move any faster. I watch all the other people disappearing into the buildings and know that the bell has rung. Then I realize I don't know where to go for my first hour class and that my class schedule is in my locker. You guessed it. I can't remember the combination to my locker. It has been years since I was a student in any school but I still have this dream. It began again more strongly when my own children began school. It was not them that I worried about being late, but me. In real life I don't remember ever actually being late to a class.

Several other people have told me that they have similar dreams about school, getting in the wrong class and everybody laughing at them, or coming to school in a hurry and finding they are still dressed in their pajamas.

My undressed dreams center in the church. I begin to walk down the aisle to find my seat in church and realize that all I have on is my slip. I never get out of these dreams with any solution. I just keep walking down that church aisle in my slip while everybody stares.

I guess my oddest dreams are when I am awake. I can fantasize all sorts of unreal things. My wide-awake dreams usually place me as a star in some complex situation that only my special talents will untangle. These dreams are comforting and build up my self-esteem greatly . . . but are often completely untrue.

In fact I even can dream that someone out there would be interested in reading about my dream life. I guess I was caught in the middle of one of my daydreams again.

HIGHWAY CONVERSATIONS
Memories of Family Travels

Several years ago when we were on a vacation trip, we spent several anxious hours on the top of Pikes Peak, waiting for Michael to make it to the top on his solo hike up the mountain. We had been misled by people at the bottom about the time and effort this hike would take. After we motored to the top to pick him up, we found that we had been quite foolish to let him start out alone. However, just at dusk he finally appeared as a speck on the trail. Lester ran down to walk the last part with him. He was near exhaustion due to the altitude, the cold, and the long, long trail.

On recounting the story to friends later, they remarked that it must have been a horrible ordeal for us. We replied that, on the contrary, it was one of the nicest parts of the trip. It was the first time in years that the teenaged son had appeared to be glad to see his parents!

Traveling with the family brings extra bonuses such as this because you are forced to talk and play and laugh with your own family while there are no other people around who care about you.

By the time you have returned from a two-week trip, you either all hate each other violently, or you have discovered that the family isn't so bad after all. The togetherness of riding in a car all day and then sleeping in a six-by-nine trailer together at night, with very few breaks in between, can really be interesting or frustrating.

One trip we took with only our two youngest children was to be a chance for Lester to get away from the phone and demands of the church. We got along pretty well and the children even found out that the old folks could be pretty good company—if there was no one else to turn to.

We reached one period of panic, however, when for two days we were up in the mountains where the radio signals from the pop music stations couldn't reach us. Since Mark didn't care for country western music, this was hard on him. For two days he switched stations, flipped dials, and then gave up every fifteen minutes. We were in such desolate country that we couldn't even play the alphabet game with signs because there were no signs. Nor could we count cows and horses because they were so few and far between. In a fifty-mile drive, we would get only to five.

There's a limit to how long you can sleep in such a situation, and since the driver naturally had to stay awake, we were driven to conversation with the family. It's amazing what you can learn about someone you have lived with for years when you begin to talk! Barriers went tumbling down and sometimes a question was even answered with two or three words instead of a grunt and a nod.

By the time we were into our third week, we had worked up to whole sentences exchanged every few minutes, even between Mark and Susan who actually seemed to enjoy talking to each other.

Lester and I congratulated ourselves on this achievement. Never again would our meals at home be silent, because we had learned how to talk to each other.

With this big glow of satisfaction, we turned into the parsonage drive late one afternoon, anticipating a nice homecoming meal together in our spacious kitchen instead of our cramped trailer.

Five minutes after we arrived and the car was released from the trailer, Mark had an errand to the highway and informed us he could grab a bite out there.

Susan spotted a playmate down the block and ran off to visit with her before we could say anything.

That night at mealtime Lester ate while scanning the mail. Susan gulped her meal to hurry back to her friends. Me? I sat in total exhaustion watching our newfound communication dissolve before my eyes.

Oh well, we did talk for two weeks. Maybe someday again someone will say something inside the house. Even to a family member!

(Note: Thirty years later these same people drive hundreds of miles to see each other and talk on the phone for hours—even to Lester and me.)

WHAT'S THAT YOU SAY?

Devout members of the congregation can sometimes change the spirit of a meeting without realizing what they have done. There was one wonderful person who was so sincere in what she said that she didn't always say what she intended to say.

In one meeting where she was conducting a program, she was earnestly urging us all to study and learn more from our lessons. Her point was that we were like little children who were easily diverted from a serious subject. In fact, she firmly told us that not many members of our congregation had reached spiritual *maternity*.

I am sure she was correct in that because we instantly began to exchange glances and smiles as we pondered her words. My friend sitting next to me whispered that she imagined the only one who had was Mary.

About the time we were getting our composure back, she again urged us to deeper thoughts, and for that purpose she asked us to take a few moments for silent *medication*. My friend again broke me up by digging in her purse to offer me an aspirin while forming the shush sound with her lips.

Our leader that day in her sincere way left us with an important message in spite of her misuse of the words.

I have been to hundreds of other meetings that were put on with perfection and beauty. But I don't remember the message of very many of them. But I will never forget the message that Jane was giving us that hot day in August. Because of her mistakes, we remembered clearly. Even when at the end of the meeting she asked us to pray with her in all *humidity*.

Several years before Lester became a minister, we had moved into a new town. Because we had a new baby, I was a very nervous mother. Since Lester had the stress of changing careers and helping me with Michael, we had not started going to any church. There was one church right across the street from our home. Since it was summertime with open windows, we could hear every word that preacher said while we were right in our living room. We were not impressed.

One evening two men from The Methodist Church (that was the correct name then) came to our door to invite us to come to their church. One of the men was a banker whom we had met. He was very articulate and accustomed to talking in public and meeting new people. The other man was one of the owners of the grocery store in town. We had seen him at the store and become acquainted with him there, but our talk was usually about the weather, comments about our baby, or help in finding what we needed in the store.

It seemed that Pete, the grocer, was the one designated to be the spokesperson in our home. We later knew that in these visitation efforts, the pairs usually took turns being the main speaker.

Pete had a hard time getting started and the words were not coming easily to him. He began to be very nervous and was actually sweating a little as he tried to tell us that their church had a good program, and he thought we would enjoy coming there. The banker said very little. When they left, he said he hoped we would consider coming to their church.

The next Sunday we attended The Methodist Church. We thought that if the church meant enough to Pete that he would come talk to us about it when it was so obviously hard for him, then it must be a place where we should be.

We might have also gone if the banker had done the talking, but we have always been glad that Pete was our spokesperson. He was the reason we ended up becoming Methodists, and we have never regretted it.

Those who are not as able to speak well many times send a stronger message than those with a golden tongue.

CAN YOU HEAR ME NOW?

Do you ever feel that after you've heard a conversation you didn't understand a word of it? You wonder if maybe you've slipped a cog or lost your marbles, because you see the lips moving and hear the words, but you don't understand a thing that has been said.

This happens to me when I am listening to an insurance agent explaining the advantages of one policy over another. By the time I plow through the annuities, the premiums, the benefits, and the beneficiaries, I'm not sure of anything except the agent's name. And that's only because he left a card with his name neatly printed for me.

Another time when you feel like a stranger from another world is when you're listening to a conversation between two people of the same profession, such as two doctors discussing a patient. With all the medical series on television recently, we are beginning to know some of the terms the doctors use, but they can really outwit us when they write it down. Even a freshman English teacher couldn't decipher the words on paper and get meaning from them.

At first I felt this way when I heard two ministers talking or informed lay people discussing church policies. I thought charge meant a courtesy a store would extend if you didn't want to immediately pay for a purchase. I knew what a conference was, of course. It was two or more people discussing something. A circuit was something to do with electricity. And an appointment was a date with a doctor or dentist. But in the talk I heard after entering the world of Methodism, a charge is the church or churches where a minister is appointed to serve. A circuit is an arrangement where several churches are combined under one preacher who goes from one to the other to minister to the people. A conference is either a geographical area that is governed by a bishop, or it is the official meeting of those in that area, unless it has another name such as general or charge put in front of the word. Those added words change the area of the official meeting. Understand? I didn't for a long time.

Along this line, I wonder what George Washington would think if he could come back and pick up a copy of the *Daily News*. If he looked at the sports page, he might really think the country was in bad shape. For example, he might read that the Washington Redskins slaughtered the Kansas City Chiefs or even more puzzling, White Sox lose star in draft. Imagine his concern for the nation if he didn't know the terms being used.

This same type of conversational gap can happen when you get in a conversation with a teenager. Recently I was talking to a sixteen-year-old about another boy who was described as a redneck. Since I wasn't sure exactly what a redneck was, I asked for an explanation. "Oh, you know, a redneck is sort of like a country hard hat." I weakly replied that I thought they were called goat ropers. I was really wrong. "Why, a goat roper is the kind of guy who drives around in a pickup truck with a gun on a rack across the back window. A redneck is short-haired and narrow-minded."

The worst offense I make with younger people is to mention that a young person has a hickey on his face. I innocently mean that they have a small pimple. The kids either react in horror or die laughing at me. It seems hickey has a meaning that is entirely different these days.

Some terms remain the same. Square still means approximately the same, except different types of people fit into that square. Keen, cute, and icky are understood by all generations but not used too often by the youngsters. But dumb and bad no longer are insults to the young, and a boy can be described as beautiful these days with no reflection on his manliness. A few years back if you called a star football player a beautiful person, you'd end up flat on your back. Now you'll get an approving pat on the back.

When you hear someone described as gross, plastic, a freak, or a jock, don't get uptight or expect anyone too different. He'd be as normal as the "It Kid," "Zoot Suiter," "BMC," or even the drip or egghead of former generations.

You don't understand me? Sorry about that. I sorta flipped and went too far out. Maybe this isn't my thing. Well, twenty-three skidoo.

I DIDN'T CATCH THE NAME

The world would be a much simpler place if people didn't have names—for example, if everyone was known as Owsley—or Hubert, no matter who he was. It would save much embarrassment for people like me who can't remember names.

Moving from church to church, with several changes in my own jobs and the children's friends, I became overwhelmed with the need to remember everyone's name.

I can meet a friend, or a former acquaintance, and be able to tell you that he has three brothers and two sisters, and that he traded his old Ford off last month just before his youngest child got the chickenpox. But I can't come up with his name. If I could just say, "Hi there, Owsley, old friend," no one would know that I have this terrible problem. But as it is, I stumble around and call him everything but his correct name, hoping it will flash into what's left of my brain before we part. It usually doesn't.

Some have told me to use association to remember the names. I tried that. It worked pretty well if I could remember what I had associated with the name. However, when I introduced a Mr. Hogsett as Mr. Pigsett, I gave up trying that method.

I even have trouble with my own children. I usually run down the list a couple of times before I latch onto the right name for the right child. They take it nicely until I have to run through the dogs' and cats' names before I settle on one. This sort of shakes their confidence in me. I have compromised in my children's names, however, and usually call both boys a combination of their two names and both the girls a combination of theirs. This makes each of them feel I may really remember them. But sometimes I can't even get those names in my mind and include some of my brothers or sisters in my vocal remembering. This usually happens when I have had a visit from one of my siblings.

Introductions can be terrible. If I am walking with a friend I have been with all day and run into an equally well-known woman and start to introduce them to each other, often I end up saying, "Hi there! Say, I want you to meet one of my dearest friends here. She really means the world to me, and I want you two to meet." I end up not using either name and hope that neither of them has noticed this. I then hope neither will ask, "What did you say her name was?"

When I associate two people together, like a mother and daughter or two close friends, I am likely to use the name of the opposite side of the pair instead of the right one. Sometimes if I can back up and repeat the first name, the last one will follow. But not always.

What really throws me is to run into someone I know quite well—but to meet this person in the wrong place. If I run into a friend from Butler when I am in Nevada, I furiously scan through my mental bank to remember which old friend she is. Then I notice she's someone from the present, not the past. But she was in the wrong place for my mentality.

So you see, it would really be so much simpler to have everyone called Owsley. No first, last, or middle names allowed. Just Owsley. You can make it appear more intimate by the tone of your voice, if necessary, but most of us have pet words for those dear to us that we use instead of names.

I mentioned this just the other day to . . . Oh, you know who I mean. Oh, what's his name? You know—my husband. Oh yes, I mentioned it to him, and he thought it would be a good idea also. Good old Owsley. He never lets me down.

SIDE EFFECTS MAY CAUSE VOCABULARY LAPSES

Jell-O again! What is the earliest commercial you can remember clearly? I'm not sure it was the very first, but the "Call for Phillip Morris" by Johnny was a great influence in my life. I never bought a Phillip Morris, but I sure tried to imitate the call. All through the neighborhood, boys would impress each other and their girls with their rendition of the phrase. That, joined with a fair imitation of Tarzan's yell, was enough to set a boy up in the eyes of his peers for a year.

Another big influence was the Burma Shave commercials that entertained our family as we drove across the country yearly. The familiar yellow-orange signs (later they were red) were watched for eagerly. We all read each one out loud. In those days of hot dusty roads and rolled-down windows, the one that stuck in my mind the most was, "Don't stick—Your elbow—Out too far—It may go home—In another car—Burma Shave." This message would spread out over half a mile or more with the few words on each small separate space sign. This was before the days of ecology and worry about signs messing up the landscape. To my eyes, those signs gave me a much bigger lift than the prettiest view! Again I have never bought Burma Shave and don't recall even what the package looked like.

I have even seen religion presented through the use of advertisements. "God is like Coca-Cola. It's the Real Thing." "God is like Hallmark. He cares enough to send the very best." "Faith is like an American Express Card. Don't leave home without it." And "God is like Duz. Duz does everything."

In thinking of brands, it seemed to me in my childhood that the really nice families all had certain brand name items in their homes. We almost looked down on people who didn't have a Hoover vacuum, a Singer sewing machine (White machine owners were sort of accepted), a Frigidaire refrigerator, and a Perfection range. These same nice people used Palmolive soap (pronounced *pal-MOL-ive*, which disguised the meaning of the name) to bathe with, Chipso to wash dishes with, and Maytags to wash their clothes in. I assume they used soap in the Maytags, but I can't really remember that brand.

It was quite a shock to me as I grew up to discover that you could be a good American and use other brands. I even switched myself and didn't get a black eye when I did.

The youngsters today watch so many commercials that I'm fairly sure they will have a more rounded view of commerces than I did. In fact, when they can't believe they ate the whole thing and realize it's not nice to fool Mother Nature, they will probably say, "Please Mother, I'd rather do it myself," as she reaches for a calming, soothing Pepto Bismal to feel good again before Mother gets Excedrin headache No. 3. And since you only get one chance at life and have to grab all the gusto while you can, then it's hard to realize that Trix are for kids.

Even finicky Maurice knows you can't eat just one, 'cause there's a new you coming every day.

It's hard to tell how many of these ads become a part of our personality, our talk, and our thoughts. It's been a long time since the song, "Super Suds, Super Suds, Lots more suds with Super Su-u-uds," hit the airwaves. The beautiful song, "I'd like to give the world a Coke," is a far cry from the early singing commercials, but each, in its way, becomes part of us in time.

If you don't believe me, spend a few days listening to others talking. See if you don't recognize many old or new commercial slogans. It's an interesting experiment. Try it, you'll like it! Can you hear me now?

HELP IS JUST A PHONE CALL AWAY

The telephone is a wonderful invention. I don't see how earlier generations existed without this machine. It has more great powers than many of us imagine possible. We all know the benefits of being able to pick up a phone and hear the voice of someone thousands of miles away. We also know the possibilities granted to us in this modern age, through the telephone, to access the Internet. These are gifts not to be taken lightly.

But now I am more interested in singing the curative powers of the telephone. I'm not feeling very well today, and I know all I have to do is go to the phone, call the doctor's office to make an appointment. Within minutes I will be feeling much better. I even hesitate to keep the appointment because I am afraid I will be seen as a hypochondriac. Just the action of making the call sets the healing motions in play, and I am much better.

When our children were little, and doctors actually made house calls, I was embarrassed more than once by making a very early morning call to the doctor after having spent the night at a sick child's bedside. After I made the call, and the doctor actually arrived, the child had rallied and was running around the house, showing no symptoms of the long night's ordeal. This was especially embarrassing to me when the doctor was a member of our congregation and I had to let him see our messy house with the sick child on the couch in the living room.

The telephone's powers are not restricted to ailing humans, however. When an appliance in your home goes on the blink, you call a repairman. When the repairman arrives, the refrigerator, computer, or furnace has become bored with its rest period and is merrily humming away with no hitches.

Calling the garage because a car has a funny noise under the hood miraculously eliminates the funny noise. When you arrive at the garage, the car runs as smoothly as can be. Even larger problems with machinery can be fixed this way also.

When professional people whose job it is to cure problems are called, it is awkward to not have the problem anymore, but at least they get paid for their trouble. But when it is your husband or wife who is called and the phone fixes the problem, it can cause real stress in a marriage.

This phenomenon makes me curious. Has the fact that we are able to turn the problem over to a professional through our phone call relieved us to the extent that we no longer notice the problem? Or in an isolated situation, such as being alone with a sick child or being afraid of having car trouble, does our imagination get the better of us, causing us to create our own problems with our worries? Miraculously, those worries disappear when we know help is on the way.

Telephones become more and more important to children as they grow into the teen years. The creation of the cell phone makes it possible for everyone to be in touch with anyone at a moment's notice. Except that the line will probably be busy.

I remember the excitement we had in our farm home when the party line phone would give two shorts and a long—our ring—and we'd race to the phone to see who was calling. It was a big occasion, and the only signs of a telemarketer would be someone calling to tell us about a basket dinner or ice cream supper that was going to be held soon. Those calls were very welcome, especially to us kids who loved to attend community affairs.

Later when we had dial phones, every ring was intended for our house, unless someone had a wrong number, but it was still a nice feeling to know a friend was calling. For a while after the dial phones were installed, we were actually on party lines but didn't hear the other rings. Therefore you could pick up the phone to use it and find that your neighbor was having a conversation with his mother. There were rules that you should talk for only five minutes so that you wouldn't tie up the line. There was also the rule that if someone had an emergency, everyone else should hang up and leave the line free. Some emergencies were no worse than trying to catch your husband before he left the office to tell him to bring home a loaf of bread.

It was a rare person who would yield the phone for an emergency call who wouldn't quietly pick up the receiver in a few seconds to hear what the emergency was all about. We could tell ourselves we wanted to be sure we weren't needed somewhere to help out, but it was usually just curiosity.

Yes, the telephone does have curative powers. It keeps us in touch with others and that is what makes us a part of the human race. We exist in community and that brings health and happiness.

But I don't think I'll call the doctor. I already feel better just writing about the call.

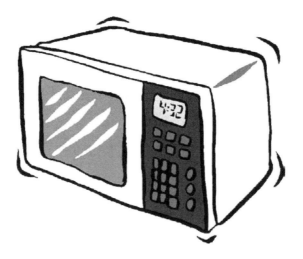

WHAT'S FOR SUPPER?

When I was a working mom with four children at home, I came home from work and started getting supper for the family. The problem was that the high school children often had to eat early or came late for supper after some school function. My minister husband likewise often had an early meeting at the church or a late unexpected hospital call to make. I also had commitments in the evening sometimes and occasionally left potpies or fish sticks for the kids while Lester and I attended a dinner somewhere. I used to think how nice it would be to have a smaller number of people to feed and have more regular hours.

Now we are retired. There are just two of us to eat meals. We have the benefit of a microwave that we didn't have back when our family was all at home. So mealtime should not be a problem, right? Wrong.

We don't have regular hours now that we are retired. There is no reason to get up early most days, but some days one or the other of us has an early morning meeting or needs to leave for an out-of-town event some distance away. Then to complicate matters, each of us occasionally has trouble sleeping. When that happens, one gets up and works on the computer or reads until sleepiness comes again. Then there may be another long nap.

So what do we do about breakfast? We each get our own when it fits our needs. No problem there until it is time for our next meal. Shall we have it at the usual time even though one has just eaten breakfast a couple hours ago? Or do we delay eating and just have one big meal in the middle of the afternoon? You can imagine that I don't need to be persuaded to make that choice. But it does cause some problems when friends or family drop by. Who expects to interrupt a meal at three p.m.?

I think back to meals when I was a child at home. Breakfast could be at various times, but it was only cooked once. We ate it then or we ate it cold. When you like biscuits and gravy as well as I do, you try to eat it while it is hot. At the farm in the summer our main meal was at noon. And that meant twelve noon. If field work kept one of the boys away at noon, it was the job of one of his sisters to take food to the field for him. Supper was always at six p.m. It was usually leftovers from the noon meal in the summer. In the winter when we lived in Washington, D.C., the six p.m. supper was the big meal. A child, who worked later or had a late class or an early date, either ate a meal that had been left in the oven or scrounged for a bite somehow.

After my father retired, I think my parents kept the same schedule for meals except that they did eat out more often. That didn't carry over to my generation. I have said often that I married for better or worse but not for lunch. Getting into the routine of preparing three meals a day never came easy. But, of course, I never was the good cook my mother was.

What I can't figure out is why we each are overweight when our mealtimes are so crazy.

THOSE HAZY, LAZY DAYS OF SUMMER BRING CHALLENGES

This must be a very good year for growing things. The fields are full of brown-eyed Susans and Queen Anne's lace. The day lilies are still blooming in lawns and along roadsides, hanging baskets of petunias grace many patios and porches, and the rose of Sharon bushes are beginning to put forth their colorful blooms. But even more abundant than these favorite flowers are the luxurious plants—vines of poison ivy. I don't think I have ever seen a year where so many areas are filled with the shiny green leaves. They crop up in the area around the base of our bigger trees where I can't get close enough with the mower to whack them down. They join my flowers in the corners by the house. They are ready to snuggle up with the *Kansas City Star* that is thrown by our mailbox instead of being placed in the slot under the box provided for newspapers. And every fence post, blackberry bush, or wild plum tree has the poison ivy hazard built in.

When I was a child, I used to get poison ivy so severely that my eyes would swell shut and my legs would be a mass of seeping sores and bumps. Then I went through a period where I didn't have the problem anymore. Perhaps I had become wiser in spotting the perpetrator before it struck me. I can remember one elementary school teacher who drilled into our class the little phrase, "When three leaves see, turn and flee." This was delivered along with a lecture at the end of the school term about dangers we might find during the summer. She covered such things as water safety, risky bicycling practices, drinking lots of water, and looking on our bodies for ticks. But she kept coming back to her chant about poison ivy. I suspect she was one who had bad experiences with the weed.

Now that I am many years out of elementary school, as I work on the riding mower, I find myself repeating the phrase with vengeance as I cut off many of the plants. I know I am risking exposure even on the mower, but I wear socks, long pants, and long sleeves.

In spite of my precautions, I recently got another very bad case. I thought I had watched carefully as I was pulling weeds in preparation for our family reunion, but somewhere along the way I came in contact with the ominous three leaves. It hit me first on my inner arm from my wrist to my elbow. Then the upper left leg on which I had rested my arm became infected. I couldn't wear my watch on my left arm because of the rash, so I changed it my right arm. Bad mistake. The watch must have brought with it some of the poison because soon that arm also became covered with rash. When it began creeping from my extremities to my body, I decided that enough was enough and sought medical help. That worked, stopping the spread and the itch, but I still hesitated to hold my two-and-one-half-month-old great-grandson at the reunion for fear of exposing his tender skin to my ailment.

Now I am hoping that having such a bad case will cause me to be immune again for a while. In the past I have had the experience of several years respite between bad cases. I have gotten a case in the winter when we tried to transplant a dormant tree. I have broken out with poison ivy when all I did was walk in the smoke of a burning brush pile. Probably one of the worst cases I received was when I took my class of Vacation Church School children on a nature hike to collect leaves and the doctor's son asked me to carry his leaves back for him because he got tired. I accused the doctor of building up business through his son when the leaves, which turned out to be poison ivy, infected me badly enough for me to seek medical help for the first time. (He didn't reduce my fee a bit either, even though he was a member of the church.)

So while we are enjoying all the beauty of the flowers that are so profuse this year, I guess we will have to accept that other species of plant life have also flourished with the proper division of rain and sun. As a side effect, it has also been a good year for chiggers and ticks. Our greedy souls yearn for a season that is filled with beauty but doesn't have the negative things associated with the growing season. We wish we could be entitled to live stress-free lives as far as Mother Nature is concerned. But even if we stay inside and enjoy only artificial plants, we still must deal with spiders and dust mites.

I know they each have their place in the scheme of things even if we don't always understand it. George Washington Carver found hundreds of good things about the peanut. I wish someone could help me find even one good thing about poison ivy, ticks, and chiggers. I'm itching to know more about them.

IT'S EASY TO GET ALL KEYED UP THESE DAYS

How old were you when you first carried a key to your home? I was reading recently about the present day *latchkey children*. These are the ones who arrive home before any of the adults in the family are present so they wear a key on a string around their necks so that they can open up the door to their own homes.

When I was the age of these children, the only key I wore around my neck was the key that fastened my roller skates to the soles of my shoes. My mother was usually home when I got home from school, but if she happened to be out, the door wasn't locked anyway. This was in Washington, D.C., and even there, in the 30s and 40s, we didn't worry about theft or vandalism. In the summers back in Vernon County, we never locked the house until the summer was over and we headed back to Washington again. Then we locked the door with a big skeleton key. A neighbor kept the key through the winter.

We did need a key to drive the car, however, but we had just the one key, which we put on the clock shelf when we were the ones who returned the car to our driveway. In Washington, we had a spot on a window seat where we left the car keys between trips. In our large family of eight children and two parents, we had only one car and only one set of keys. I don't remember any problems about scheduling the use of the car, but I am sure my older siblings could come up with memories about that. By the time I was driving age, there were just two of us left at home, and we often went places together in the car.

Even after my parents retired back to the farm full-time, they didn't give each of us our own key to our house. We could enter whenever we happened to be near. We each were told where a key was hanging and then could enter as we wished. By then they had installed a different type of lock that required the smaller keys as we have today. But I don't remember the door being locked unless they were off on a short trip someplace.

When I was in college, girls had certain hours they were required to be back in their dorms or rooming houses. The landlady was required to lock the doors at ten o'clock Monday through Thursday nights, eleven o'clock on Sunday, and twelve on Friday and Saturday. We had no keys of our own to our rooms or the house. If we needed to be out later than the prescribed hours, we had to have permission and the landlady would either leave the door unlocked or get up to let us in. This happened to me after Lester was in the army. I wanted to meet him when he came back on a short leave. The bus didn't get in before closing hours, but my landlady relented and let me meet him anyway. It turned out he missed the bus, so I had to walk the darkened streets of Columbia alone at midnight. It was the only time I was ever frightened by being alone because some boys kept tailing me in a car and calling out to me. I was very glad to find an unlocked door when I reached Matthews Street. (Lester arrived very early the next morning.)

Fast forward a generation and Lester and I lived in various parsonages with our four children during each stage of their lives. None of them can remember having a key to our home until they were old enough to also carry a car key. None of them had a car of their own until they had left home, but we did have several keys for the family cars.

The freedom to come and go while not being afraid to leave possessions unguarded was just a natural occurrence in my life until more recent years. I regret that my grandchildren will never have experienced such freedom. I know there must have been burglaries happening in those days, but I guess our neighborhoods weren't considered rich enough for any of us to fear being robbed.

Now I have a key for our car, for our truck, for several doors on the house, for the family house across the field, and until recently, I also carried keys for the places where I worked. Since I now work out of my home, those keys are eliminated. Our kids do know how to enter our home if no one is here, since they are quite a bit too old to be wearing keys on strings around their necks.

The freedom of my youth and early adulthood has been locked away in my memory. In reality in these middle age plus years, I not only have the restriction of feeling I must lock things up, but I have a worse restriction.

When I get things locked up safely, I have trouble remembering where I put the key. Even when I know it is in my purse, I can have a game of hide-and-seek with myself as I rummage through the interior of my ample bag. This is particularly frustrating when a carryout person from the grocery store is patiently waiting to load my food in the car. In my anxiety, I realize I need a Kleenex for a dripping nose. Then I find I had put my keys in my pocket and not in my purse after all. Maybe I should get a long string for my neck.

LET ME TELL YOU . . .

When people are gone on vacation, they have much fun visualizing how interested everyone will be to hear all that is happening on the trip. They picture entertaining evenings sitting around in neighborhood homes telling breathless audiences all about their narrow escapes with full campsites and dirty restrooms.

It is quite a blow to return home and find that most of the people hadn't even realized you were gone. Of course, the church people wondered why there was a substitute preacher for two Sundays, but they didn't know why. Those who did notice you were gone were not at all interested in what you did or where you went. After a few polite questions, they immediately launch into all the details of what you missed right here at home while you were gone.

Never had the old town been as exciting as the period you chose to be gone. Parties, picnic, meetings—all were held in quantities and everyone had a glorious time. The weather was either the best it had been in years, and you missed it all by being gone, or the weather was the worst we've ever experienced, and you won't get to report it to your grandchildren because you were way out west and missed it all.

So now you are left with hundreds of tales of travel and dozens of beautiful photographs and no one really cares about them. There is one exception. That is the person who has already taken the same trip you just returned from. He will listen closely to any tales you have about your journey. He listens intently so he can find the first pause in your breath to jump in and tell how it was last year when he was there.

Another favorite with those who have passed that way before is to point out that you missed the really best parts of all that you visited. Invariably the parts you chose to pass over were the ones that made the biggest impression on them, and they will tell you at length that you were pretty foolish, if not downright stupid, to have overlooked the choice things to see.

Some might be interested in finding out what the trip cost you, how many miles you drove each day, and what were the best places to eat.

We usually can't tell much about good eating places, unless you consider McDonald's and Dairy Queen as gourmet food. We usually keep track of the costs but don't have the nerve to add up the totals, and the number of miles we travel in a day can fluctuate greatly. When we first start out, we take our time, stop to see sights, call it a day in late afternoon, and just take it easy. When we turn toward home, we are like the proverbial horse who races when it is turned toward home. We drive from early morning until late night to cover those miles and get home.

Which makes you wonder . . . if we are so eager to get home, why did we leave in the first place?

GIVING BIRTH TO TRADITIONS

I didn't often accompany Lester as he made his hospital rounds visiting the church members who were ill. But often when a new baby was born, I would go with him to the hospital. Then I would see the new mother the day of her firstborn's birth. She would be resting in the hospital bed with many people caring for her needs. This shows how confused our world is. Any mother of a child older than one year knows that the time a mother needs hospital rest and care is on the anniversary of the child's birth.

I refer, of course, to the ritual of THE BIRTHDAY PARTY.

Early birthday parties are delightful affairs of tears because paper hats are thrown into melted ice cream. Tears because the guest does not want to part with his prettily wrapped gift. Tears because the young host refuses to share his new (or old) toys with his guest. Spilled pop. Wet pants. Stained rugs. And finally, tears of entreaty as the parents of the host plead with their offspring to please come out of the closet and play with his friends.

Recuperation for the parents requires approximately a week.

The parents of children in the lower grades have an entirely different experience. The crescendo of noise at a party builds steadily from the shriek of delight when the first guest arrives until the blessed doorbell ring that announces the last parent has come to claim a guest. Any child who is not running and/or yelling is undoubtedly in tears because he or she (1) has been left out of a game, (2) didn't win a game, (3) has a bloody nose, (4) has a stomachache, or (5) someone else beat him to the bathroom. Gifts are appraised with experienced eyes and guests can quickly inform their hosts how the loot compares with that of the last birthday child in the group.

Recuperation time for the parents varies between one and two weeks.

The preteen years allow the parents a few years of partial bliss. The guests and hosts have each learned a few social graces. Amusement is handled by the kids themselves and usually ranges between showing prowess at burps and food consumption (boys), and giggles and food consumption (girls). Hurt feelings and bruises are rare and there is even some mild enthusiasm for the parents' attempts at entertainment.

Recuperation takes only one day.

Early teenage parties can become horrors of (1) girls lining one wall with the hosts imploring the boys to leave the opposite wall and join in the *fun,* or (2) boys and girls pairing off and trying to disappear from the group, and (3) food and drinks running out every fifteen minutes.

Recovery time for the parents can come in approximately two weeks.

Then comes the sweet sixteen birthday time. The only party desired is at city hall with the state patrol driving examiner. Once that is accomplished, the house is empty and quiet. The only sound on the sixteenth birthday anniversary is the nervous walking up and down the room by the father and the swish of the curtains as the mother looks to the street for the seventeeth time. Then, finally, the sigh of relief by each parent when the sound of brakes, car doors, and laughter outside signal the safe arrival home.

Recovery for the parents from the sixteenth birthday party usually comes in about ten years. Then the young person begins to worry about the old folks and their driving abilities.

4

LOOK AT ME NOW!

Will the meeting come to order?
(I now can hold the gavel
On committees, boards, and agencies
And even get to travel.)

A COMMUNITY OF WOMEN

The Purpose of the United Methodist Women, which is said at each meeting of the organization, contains the phrase, "The organized unit of United Methodist Women shall be a community of women whose purpose is to know God." This group has been very important in my journey of finding a place in the new life I faced when Lester became a minister. Since I was not *into* a lot of worshipful practices and was quite freethinking in my theology, I was afraid that I would be a deterrent to Lester's ministry.

When we went to his first appointment in Archie, the United Methodist Women had not yet been organized. But two of its predecessor organizations were very active. One was called the Women's Society of Christian Service, which met in the daytime with mainly older women attending. The other was The Wesleyan Service Guild, which was organized for women who were employed outside the home. However, some younger women who were not employed outside the home also belonged to it.

I thought I should join both organizations as a good wife should, and I have never been sorry. The acceptance I found in each group made my transition to parsonage life much easier than I expected. But, even more importantly, the work of these two units, nationwide, opened up a new approach for me to the Christian life. I had always been interested in social work, and I saw these groups doing social work on a worldwide basis. Only they called it Mission.

In a few years these two organizations merged into one, the United Methodist Women, when the United Brethren denomination joined with The Methodist Church to become The United Methodist Church. By then we were living in another town, and the strong United Methodist Women's group there got me started into going beyond the local church for events and training.

Eventually, I became a district officer, then a conference officer and later had the great experience of being a jurisdiction officer where I had contact with hundreds of women of different ethnic and economic backgrounds. I had the heady experience of being vice-president, which put me in charge of a large jurisdiction meeting of some 600 women who gathered in Dallas for training, celebration, and study. I also was elected as a jurisdictional delegate to the conference, which elects bishops and carries on the business of the church.

So here I was no longer on the sidelines but walking hand in hand with national leaders of our denomination. I now understood the scope of our work, both in the United Methodist Women as well as The United Methodist Church. I was proud to be a part of what went on.

Later I was elected president of our own Missouri West Conference United Methodist Women and felt the love and support of hundreds of women as we worked together to be this community of women whose purpose is to know God.

Did I forget to tell you that I had a lot of fun doing all of these things? Women and men who are leaders in the church take their work seriously, but they can have lots of fun while they are doing it. One of my favorite UMW members coined this little poem about our group:

Mary had a little lamb
She could have been a sheep
But she joined UMW
And died from lack of sleep.

CAREER ROLLER COASTER RIDE

A common complaint of ministers' spouses is the problem of having their own careers while the minister is moving from church to church. In my case, I started doing substitute teaching when my children got past the baby stages. This was something I could do to boost our income wherever we were. Often I was the main substitute and would be called for everything from kindergarten to high school chemistry. (I was better in the kindergarten classes.)

The main drawback to this occupation was that it was hard on the children of our congregation. Since I was always active as a youth group leader in every church Lester served, I was good friends with most of the children and youth. Therefore, when I walked into a class and saw some of *our* kids there, I would count on them to help me get things straight. The usual tricks that students play on substitutes wouldn't work if my friends clued me in. Of course, that didn't make them very popular with their peers. Though I tried not to put them on the spot too often, I was always glad to see them in any class.

Because of the education I received in United Methodist Women, I became very interested in social work and spent over twenty-five years doing some form of that work in the various locations. This began when I was what was then called a child welfare worker in the Bates County Welfare Office. In our next location it took a couple of years before I was able to get any full-time position in my chosen field. In the meantime, I spent three months as a dispatcher in the sheriff's office and did the trusty substituting jobs again. Finally, I was hired at Interfaith Community Services in Saint Joseph (called Inter/Serv) with the title of church in action coordinator. This was perfect in that it combined my contacts through the church, through United Methodist Women, and my background in social work. The United Methodists, Presbyterians, United Church of Christ, and Catholics sponsored this agency at that time with much participation from the Jewish community.

One of my responsibilities in this job was to coordinate the Christmas Store a few days before Christmas for the low-income persons to come choose gifts for their families. Churches and businesses, in cooperation with the Salvation Army, donated money and items to make this store possible. But what was most meaningful was the group of volunteers that staffed the store. The women and men from the Jewish Tabernacle volunteered to do this work on December 24 so that the Christian volunteers could be free on that day. Standing in that large room and watching those wonderful Jewish persons wishing a "Merry Christmas" to the clients who were trying to scrape together a Christmas for their families was one of the nicest things I have experienced in my career.

After the next move, since I was too far away from Saint Joseph to continue in that work, I worked on the church staff directing a neighborhood day care and after-school program. Another move and I again found work on the church staff.

As Lester's time to retire was approaching, I had an opportunity to return home, to Nevada, and be director of a community social agency. We decided that a year of a commuter marriage would be okay since he would be retiring the next year. It turned out that an opening for Lester came up quicker at nearby Ft. Scott, Kansas, so I spent only three months commuting back to his church at Versailles, Missouri, for the weekends before he was with me full time.

After three years in this position I decided I had reached the age to retire, but after a few months, I became involved with a group trying to supply respite care in the community. We established an adult day care, which I then directed for five years.

I did retire at that time but started my writing career, which I imagine will continue for some time. When I can work from home and have lots to say, there's no reason to quit now. Unless you all get tired of reading my words!

FIRST SIGHTINGS

Recently I was coming home from two days in Jefferson City where I was attending the United Methodist Women's legislative event. I was riding with Mary Ireland, who is one of the committee members responsible for this year's program. We had been talking about how excited we were to have been able to sit at the same table with former Senator Jean Carnahan at our evening meal. We also remembered our breakfast with both Senator Harold Caskey and Representative Jerry King that we shared with others from our area. But we were each getting tired after the nonstop drive from the city. We were eager to get home.

I told Mary about our yearly trips back to Vernon County each June when I was a child. About the time we passed the Walker corner, all of our family would eagerly scan the horizon to be the first to see either the now non-existent water towers at State Hospital No. 3 or to spot the courthouse tower. Mary and I began the same game. We soon spotted the newer large blue water tower near the subway, but neither of us saw the courthouse tower until we were looking straight ahead at it when we were almost into town. Being middle age plus, I shouldn't be quite as excited about getting home as I was some seventy years ago, but the sight of the Vernon County Courthouse tower still gave me a tingle. I was home again and things appeared to be the same in my hometown.

Later Mary dropped me off at our church where Lester was meeting me. As we drove up, we saw the neighbors' lawn on College Street filled with crocus blossoms. The first blooms of spring had finally come! (When Lester and I later got out to our country home, my heart lifted again as we spotted yellow and purple crocus blooming in our own front yard.) Other flowers will come soon, but these first flowers give us hope and excitement. I began thinking about other first sightings that bring a thrill.

As a parent, grandparent, and great-grandparent, it is easy to remember the feelings the first time we see each new little one that comes into our family. Although we see them thousands of times in our lives, no memory is clearer than the very first time we saw that little face. When that little face shows a first smile, and the smile, in time, shows a first tooth, again we celebrate.

Several years later our experience is somewhat different when we see a gap in the bigger smile as the child proudly shows the loss of a first tooth. The first sight of each child getting on a school bus or entering a classroom door brings bittersweet memories of loss and pride combined. There is no end to these first sights concerning the children: the first boyfriend or girlfriend calling at the door; the first vision of a child driving off alone in a car; the first packed suitcase; and on and on. When you have more than one child, these first sightings tumble upon each other as the children reach different stages at the same time. They are still memorable, but they sometimes get a little blurred as we try to sort out time and place in our thoughts.

And thinking about first sights that get a little blurred, how about that first sight of your own gray hair, your first missing tooth in adulthood, or the first time you notice how wrinkled your hands are?

I think it is more fun to remember the crocus.

RESPONSIBILITIES ARE ASSIGNED FOR VARIOUS REASONS

We have just returned from four days of attending the annual conference of our denomination. We have attended this event in June for many years as Lester is a voting member of the body. From time to time I have been a member at large. This year I had no such designation and no responsibilities at the conference. Because of the time crunch I am experiencing with many activities and getting our family home prepared for the Gray family quadrennial reunion, I had been hesitant to follow our usual custom. We always enjoy seeing all our church friends from across the conference and keeping in touch with the newer ministers and laity that are taking their places in our group. But this year I thought I might bypass the experience and not go with Lester.

Another problem had arisen in that Michael and Mark were coming home to help us with some of the outside work of getting the farm in shape for all those who will soon be arriving. They would still be here for a day after we would need to leave to attend the meeting. Since they had come from Milwaukee and near Dallas respectively, I hated to cut short any time from their visit. They insisted that they had come to work, not to visit. (I think maybe they thought a day together without the *old folks* might even be nice.)

While I was still struggling over the decision, I received an email from a woman in the conference who was responsible for part of the worship experiences at the meeting. In the email she asked me if I would be part of the processional of the opening worship. She told me I would not need to speak but would walk up the aisle carrying some token or banner.

Well, my ego kicked in here. If she had chosen *me* to have this honor, I certainly didn't want to say no. To get there in time for the instructions for the processional, we needed to leave our home at four a.m. I had to arrive earlier than Lester needed to be there, but we both agreed I should go.

I emailed back that I would be happy to do this, and we proceeded to arrange our activities so we could make the trip. Because we didn't want to short our time with our sons, we stayed up rather late for our final visit and then got up at three-thirty to make the 200-mile drive to Columbia.

When I arrived at the room where we were to get our instructions, I found that in addition to me, there would be eighty-nine other people in the procession. The tokens we were to carry were colored balloons to designate which district of our church we were representing.

Well, it wasn't exactly a stellar role, but I smiled at my deflated ego and got in line with the others for our grand parade. I began to look at the others from our district and the other districts. In each group of four from each district, there was a youth wearing a blue tee shirt designating that each of them was a United Methodist Youth. Also in each group were a minister and the lay leader for the district. That left the role I was filling. I checked with a woman I knew in another foursome near me to see if she knew how these fourth persons were chosen. She said she thought she had figured it out by looking at each of the other groups as well as her own.

We were chosen for this role not because we were important, not because we held a certain office, not because we had any special talents for walking and carrying balloons. We were chosen because we were old.

So, leaving visiting sons at home, driving miles through the early dawn, and rushing to get my instructions all boiled down to being recognized because I was old.

We made our walk down the aisle and then took our seats in the crowded hall. I sat next to a longtime friend and told her about my experiences. She laughed with me about my delusions of grandeur and then confessed she hadn't even seen me in the processions at all. The hall was so crowded that all anyone could see was the colorful balloons.

Well, at least we got the balloons carried in okay. And if no one really saw who had been involved, maybe they didn't have to know that for one-fourth of us our only claim to fame was that we are old.

WHAT TO DO WITH EXTRA TIME HAS PROBLEMS

One of the worst things about giving up some responsibilities is that you now have more time to do other things: things that you have been putting off until you have more time; things you really didn't want to do at all. So I finished my term as president of the Missouri West Conference of United Methodist Women and declined to have my name on the slate for a second two-year term. I wanted to have more time at home.

I decided that I would tackle one of the *put-off* jobs each day until everything was brought up to tiptop shape and Martha Stewart could visit any time and not cause me embarrassment. I was going to start with something rather light that would be pleasurable—something like reading through all the old magazines to see if there was anything in them that I wanted to clip and save.

I needed to get a cold drink to refresh myself as I undertook this chore, so I went to the refrigerator to get a cold one (Dr. Pepper, that is). That was a mistake. I spilled a dish of applesauce as I was reaching past all the bowls and bottles to reach the soda. If I had to clean up that mess, I might as well start my jobs with cleaning out the refrigerator.

In *the olden days* before automatic defrosting, I had to clean the refrigerator at least every two weeks or so when I defrosted the freezer compartment. I always made enough of a mess with the dripping ice that I at least sponged out the interior fairly regularly. Now there is no need for defrosting or dripping ice so things can get pretty nasty before I notice the problem.

I began by taking out the vegetable bins and the shelf that they attach to since that is where the applesauce landed. The shelf was loaded down with cans and bottles of various sizes so I assorted them neatly by category on the kitchen island. As I reached farther back, I began to find jars of jelly with just one dab left in the bottom that now had a nice crystalline glow on it. These I filled with water and left in the sink to clean and to later recycle the jars.

When our family gathers at our home, everyone is very good at helping with the shopping, cooking, and putting away after our big meals. Many of our gathering times are planned around a picnic-type meal. Therefore, just in case, those doing the shopping get a jar of mustard, ketchup, olives, and pickles. It wouldn't be a picnic without them. But rarely do we finish a whole bottle at the gathering, so it is put back into the refrigerator for the next time. Only the next time someone probably also buys a new supply. I found four containers of mustard, three of ketchup, and thirteen bottles of either olives or pickles. Now my problem is—do I combine these jars of various time eras or throw some away and just keep those that seem to be the freshest? I couldn't make this big decision by myself so I threw away any that looked really nasty and kept the rest to neatly put back on the shelves, gathered in a designated spot for later decisions.

After throwing out several half-consumed juice, Gatorade, and soda bottles that various grandchildren or great-grandchildren had left to finish later, taking out all the shelves for a good scrubbing, and sponging down the sides of the appliance, I was ready to reassemble the shelves. I am sure that the refrigerator wasn't designed by a woman who would have to clean it. There are many little crevices in the baskets and shelves that are too small to get a washcloth into, but big enough to gather multitudes of sticky syrup or dried milk. These crevices are very important in putting everything back together again, however. If things don't fit just right, the whole thing comes a-tumbling down. Also I found that the shelves had to all be put in the same brackets on each side or everything will shift sideways. I discovered this after I had reloaded a clean but leaning shelf.

This morning I enjoyed opening the shining clean door to a sparkling interior where my pitcher of orange juice sat by cleaned jars of jelly and no bowls of applesauce anywhere in sight. I tried not to look at the thirteen jars of pickles and olives clustered on the top shelf.

Come to think of it, I never did get my cold drink nor did I read even one of the old magazines. But that is something that can be put off until another day.

Lester just came in and asked me if I knew that the watermelon that we bought for the rained-out church picnic was still in the breezeway refrigerator. He said it looked like it wasn't good anymore. That refrigerator is one we use for extra stuff like cartons of soft drinks, gallon jugs of cider, and the food our sons bring back from their canoeing trips. I rarely open it unless we have company or I have bought a really big quantity of groceries.

I guess that will be my project for tomorrow. I will empty and clean out this old refrigerator. Please pray for me.

VIPS TOGETHER

During the early years of Lester's ministry, I was very impressed with the importance of the leaders of the church. I became somewhat tongue-tied when one of the seminary professors or a district superintendent was visiting in our church or home. Gradually this changed for me until I felt that these people were my friends, and I enjoyed their company.

As I became better known throughout our conference, I was put on committees and was able to serve side by side with many of those I used to stand in awe of.

When I realized that they respected Lester and me and valued our opinions as much as we did theirs, I thought how different this had all turned out from what I had expected.

When I was lucky enough to be chosen as a voting delegate to our jurisdictional conference, I was seated next to the president of Saint Paul School of Theology in Kansas City. We were seated in the order of our election, alternating clergy and laity. I was astounded that I could be on the same level as this renowned leader. But he showed no hesitation in asking my opinion as matters came before us for a vote. I asked him hundreds of questions as this was a one-time only experience for me, and he had been through it several times. He was very patient, and I quickly learned about the mechanics of our church's organization.

I had been selected by our delegation to serve on the committee that nominates members to national boards, committees, and agencies. I sat, as the only representative of our conference, with the other sixteen representatives of their conferences, trying to get Missouri West's members named to an appropriate number of these important positions. This was intimidating, but I was helped by the fact that I had a quantity of well-qualified people to nominate.

After the process was over, I was thrilled when one of the professors from the seminary congratulated me on my work in the committee and especially thanked me for putting him in a position he wanted. To think that I had been able to help a man of his stature was a heady experience.

I remembered back to the time I was overwhelmed when Bishop Frank had greeted me by name. The fact that a bishop remembered me and remembered my name had been a highlight for me. Later bishops also knew me, some better than others, but no later greeting had the same impact as that first time.

After Lester's retirement, while I was still very active in conference United Methodist Women, we sometimes went to a meeting together where he would be introduced as Carolyn's husband. After years of being introduced as *the minister's wife*, *Lester's wife*, or even as *one of our ministers' wives*, that was a good feeling.

We each gained importance through the achievements of the other.

THOUGHTS ON MAKING A LIST

In one of my favorite Gilbert and Sullivan tunes from *The Mikado*, the lyrics tell about making a list of people who wouldn't be missed if the Lord High Executioner were forced to carry out his job. A more cheery song tells about the list that Santa Claus makes each year, checking it twice before making his Christmas deliveries. Common phrases use the word *list* to put across an idea. An example is, "He's on the short list," meaning that he has a good chance of being chosen for whatever position being talked about. Another use would be, "After what she did, she is really on my list!" That is not a favored position.

I am looking ahead to when I will be out of town teaching an Elderhostel. I began thinking about all that I should do before I leave. I decided that the best thing would be to make a list. I often use this method to get organized before a big event. I try to remember everything that I will need to take with me—what should be done at home before I leave and what preparations I want to complete ahead of time.

When we were making preparations for our big Gray family reunion in June, our son came a few days early to help with final plans. One of the first things he did was to make a list of jobs and assign them to different family members. He wrote down one task that he didn't realize I had already done. I brought this to his attention, but he put it down on the list anyway, with my name assigned to it, and then scratched a line through it. He said half of the benefit of making a list is to be able to scratch things off, one by one, as the duties get finished. So the list got shortened very quickly because I thought of several other things he could add which had been completed already.

Another time that I prepare a list is when I am deciding what groceries I need to buy on my next trip to town. As I notice I am getting low on a product or food, I jot it down on the list so that I won't forget it when I do get to the store. The one thing I usually forget is to take the list with me when I go. Maybe the action of actually writing something makes it easier to remember what I need, even if I forget the list.

Social activities bring forth the need for lists also. Weddings require much thought in who will be put on the invited list and who will only be on the announcement list. Listing attendants and choosing relatives and friends whom you would like to include is an ordeal that can cause a couple to elope instead of making the choices. In order to make this list, there must first be a list of expense and budget items. That can greatly alter the guest list as the dollar signs mount up.

After the invitations are sent and acceptances received, there is now need for another list for how to seat the family members. One list is for those who sit on the first row, another for following rows. This is especially hard when there has been a divorce and both parents or grandparents wish to attend. Then there are lists for who comes to the rehearsal dinner and numerous other events.

Many parents and school children scan the posted lists in stores to see what school supplies will be required for their grade when school starts at the new year. Most children like to add to the school's list with their own personal requirements, such as a new back-pack or the proper kind of athletic shoes. (By *proper* they mean the brand the other kids will be wearing.)

Organizations often begin their year with fresh lists of members, phone numbers, and addresses, and now their email addresses. Using last year's roster can cause embarrassing moments when there has been a name change or a change in membership. Listing officers and meeting dates and programs keeps the group well organized for the year.

So, back to my plans for listing what I should do before leaving next week. I realize that one of the things I need to do is make a list of things for family members to do while I am gone. The cats, birds, and flowers would appreciate being listed as needing attention in my absence.

Should I put such things on the list that I know I won't forget, such as pack my suitcase? It gives me one more thing to scratch off, but since I can't complete that until I am basically going out the door, it may not have too much psychological value. But maybe I'll put it there anyway. It makes me look more important to have a long list.

Now that I have written this, I can scratch off one more thing. I hope I can get through all of the others because I realize I am so tired from all this writing that I may end up being quite listless.

5

IT'S A GOOD LIFE, CAROLYN T.

I like the way my life has changed
I never thought I'd say it—
But looking back, the view is great,
And now I'm pleased to say it.

OUT TO THE AIRPORT AND DOWN THE ROAD TO GRANDMOTHER'S HOUSE WE GO

Most women understand the sense of panic that sets in a day or two before a big event is planned to take place *in their own house*. Many times something that sounded like a great idea several weeks ago when the gathering was planned suddenly looks different when the day is drawing near. Conditions in the house and yard that have looked fine all year suddenly look like they need (1) a new coat of paint, (2) new accent pieces, such as a complete set of living room furniture, or (3) a full-time housekeeper and gardener.

All year you may have lived happily with a pair of mismatched socks decorating the dryer awaiting the eventual return of a matching pair. Now that, along with a hundred other little out of place items, needs to be hidden or perhaps even returned to the place where they belong. Watermarks on the ceiling, which you have noticed only when you wake up too early in the morning, now seem to be as noticeable as neon lights. Outside attempts at a flower garden appear pitiful—seen through the imagined impression given to the eyes of a guest. In fact, everything about your home that was perfectly fine before now seems to need much TLC to meet your new, higher criteria as you await the big day.

Tomorrow I am expecting eighty-eight of my closest relatives to come for a three-day reunion at the family home. Some of them were raised in the home. Others visited there most summers of their childhood and youth. And for some it will be the first time to ever put foot on this farm that has been in our family for a century. Since my husband and I bought eighty acres of the family farm years ago, before Lester became a minister and was an extension agent here in Vernon County, we established our retirement home on this eighty, which adjoins the family farm. Since Lester has managed the farm since shortly before my father's death in 1964, we are playing the role of hosts along with our daughter Shirley, who actually lives in the family home.

The details of preparations can be time consuming, but the worry that something will be left undone is more troublesome. Did I really order the two Porta Potties or did I just think about it? When was I supposed to give the exact meal counts to the caterers? Will the sand for the beach by the new pond be delivered on time, or will the truck get stuck in the field trying to get the sand to the right place? Do we have time to cut those dead limbs out of the big oak tree, or will it make too much of a mess at this point?

Other things are out of our control, but they don't escape my worrying anyway. Can we all fit under the new carport shelter if it rains? If it stays too hot, will some of the older people have trouble adjusting to the heat? Will the people recognize poison ivy and stay away from the ominous three leaves? And will the Easterners remember that there are chiggers in Missouri?

The younger relatives who are coming *home* for the first time may wonder why everyone is so intent on revisiting this place. After all, it is just a fairly big, quite old, ordinary house in a nice lawn with lots of trees. What seems to be the big draw that causes people to arrange schedules four years in advance to be sure to be able to attend? It isn't just the tradition. It isn't just the farm that celebrates a hundred years with the Gray family this year. It isn't only the memories of summer games on the lawn, community friends who have been like part of the family, or even of the pictures and furnishings that have stayed the same in several areas of the house. No, it is the feeling that somewhere in this vastly changed world there is a spot that belongs to our family. There is a spot where we can always return and feel welcome, a spot that carries memories of a wonderful couple who created this home and became our parents, grandparents, great-grandparents and great-great-grandparents.

My mother used to worry about what would become of her beloved home after she died. Now, thirty-three years after her death, her family is still returning to share with one another, to meet the new little ones and the new in-laws, and to experience the family roots that go deeply into this Vernon County soil. These roots continue to produce a harvest of love and a sense of belonging.

While I mow down the last round of weeds and buy the last list of provisions, I will save one job until the last minute. Then I will sweep off Mama's sidewalk to the front door to let her know that I have readied her home for her kids to come home again. And Papa would be glad to know that the land he chose for his own father to buy in 1902 is still in good hands.

Oh yes, I found out. I did order the Porta Potties.

LIVING IN MAYBERRY OR DOWN THE ROAD SUITS ME JUST FINE

In November there was an article in the *Kansas City Star* about a situation in Butler. The reporter of the incident described Butler as a town where you might expect Andy and Opie to come walking down the street any moment. The brick-paved streets were described as cobblestone, which, of course, is not the same at all. With humor the town was dismissed as one that had only one stoplight. Nowhere did the reporter realize all the advantages that Butler, or any smaller town, could offer its citizens.

We lived in Butler for six years while Lester was serving the Ohio Street Church and the Mt. Zion United Methodist Church back in the 1970s. We enjoyed the town very much. With one exception every town that we have lived in throughout our fifty-seven years of marriage has been under 10,000 population. I wouldn't change any one of those towns for the city the Kansas City reporter evidently comes from.

Only one stoplight means there will be very few times when you will be caught up in a traffic snarl. It means that cars move more leisurely, and if the reporter had happened to notice, he would have seen many friendly waves from one motorist to another. The brick-paved streets around the square give a beauty to the courthouse lawn and the stores around the block. In those stores many clerks and proprietors call their customers by name. So if you would happen to see Andy and Opie walking by, it would only add to the day's pleasures.

Nevada is approximately twice the size of Butler. We have seven stoplights, but our former mayor, George Washburn, described Nevada's traffic as having a rush minute, not a rush hour. Our streets are no longer made with brick, but we do have shade trees lining many residential streets. Our courthouse lawn and the stores around the square are attractive. Casual visiting takes place within the walls of many stores. I don't know how that same reporter would describe our town, but I could tell him that I feel this is a good place to live, and its size is one of the biggest assets.

I'll admit there were times when I was a youth that I didn't really cherish the thought that half of the businesses in town knew my parents and knew who I was. I realized that any indiscretion I might commit would be reported eventually. However, that same family knowledge would help out when a flat tire or other car trouble caused me problems.

As I became middle age plus and returned to Nevada with fondness, I realized that the same sense of belonging was a big comfort to me throughout the last years of my older sister Miriam. Doctors, bankers, lawyers, neighbors, and service people lightened our burdens and shared our sadness. In our hometown, things do not have to be faced alone. We are a community.

Each time I travel to a bigger city, I have a good time. But each time I am even happier to return home.

When I go to Kansas City and get a little south of Harrisonville on the return trip, I relax and enjoy the surroundings. I pass the home of friends we had when Lester was the minister in Archie. I enjoy memories of rivalries with neighboring Adrian school teams. Then I pass Butler and its brick streets. Often I will turn off the highway and pass the one stoplight to visit a friend or stop at one of the stores.

Rich Hill offers memories of times when I was a caseworker for what was then called the Bates County Welfare Office. I was first assigned to the region around Rich Hill, and I learned to know and love many of my clients. Rich Hill doesn't even have one stoplight, but it has two beautiful parks and outstanding fireworks displays each Fourth of July.

As I come nearer to Nevada, I always look for the big billboards that tell the world about Cottey College and then later, the spirit of Nevada. Coming home from a one-day outing or an absence of several days, I always get that same rush that says, I'm home, and home is a great place to be.

I will stand up for any of the little towns that I have called home, and I challenge any reporter to spend a day with me while I show the benefits of small town living. No matter what age you are, the Mayberrys of this world are good places to live. When you are middle age plus, there is nothing any better.

MESSAGES AND INSPIRATIONS IN THE CHURCH

I have enjoyed many sermons while attending church services. Many of them have not been given from the pulpit or by the minister. Some have not even been spoken. All have been inspirational, memorable, or thought provoking.

On a recent Sunday two longtime friends were sitting together a few rows ahead of me. Being one of the first warmer days of the season, it was not warm enough to need the air conditioner. The ceiling fans brought a little coolness to the sanctuary. One of these women has had some recent health problems and is a little more frail than usual. During the service it was apparent that the fans were chilling her as she was holding her arms close to her body. Her body language told that she was cold. However, she had not made any move to put on her jacket that was behind her in the seat.

The other woman looked her way, noticed the signs of discomfort, and, without saying a word, brought the jacket up over her friend's shoulders, giving her a little pat and smile as she adjusted the garment. The immediate response was a relaxation of the rigid body, a returned smile, and a half hug to her friend.

This simple act of two friends so attuned to the needs of each other, with the ability to communicate in love without a word, took me back in memory to another place and two much younger churchgoers.

When our youngest daughter was about eighteen months old, Lester was serving the church at Archie. During a special program, the children, by classes, were to go up on the small stage and sing a song. Our Susan was the youngest in her little class. As the children reached the two steps that led up to the platform, another child, who was only a few months older than Susan, turned and took Susan's hand to help her navigate the steps. The two had played together often and Christi instinctively knew that without a little help, Susan would have had to get on her hands and knees to climb the steps. They reached the platform, still holding hands, and turned to take part in their little song. Everyone in the congregation was wearing a loving smile after observing this simple act of caring among the very youngest children.

At another church, an intergenerational act of concern and love has warmed my heart for years. We were in the church's Fellowship Hall for some event, but our youngest son, Mark, had stayed home. Susan was with us and the two older children were with the youth group in another room. A tornado had been spotted heading toward Butler, and the siren, which was very near the church, began to sound. Police cars roamed the streets with their sirens blowing.

I was concerned for Mark who was home alone and rushed to the phone to give him instructions on what to do. He seemed to be feeling okay about the situation and was watching TV in his basement bedroom. I decided that was as safe as anything I could suggest, so I turned back to the group at the church. I saw a minister friend of ours cuddling Susan over in a protected corner of the room. In my concern for Mark's being alone, I had not dealt with the fears our youngest was having right in our presence. Our friend saw her fear and turned the moment into a feeling of security instead of fright.

Another example happens at each covered dish dinner we have in our present church. Since I have an allergy to onions and garlic, a very special lady always fixes a casserole that has neither of the offending elements in it. Then at the meal she will quietly tell me ahead of time which dish I may eat without concern. There are many people in the church, but she remembers this problem of mine along with all the other things she does for many people.

These sermons come across to me loud and clear. There is no straining to hear what the minister said. Everything is simple, yet complex.

Concern for others, combined with actions that show that concern, is the backbone of any church—or for society as a whole. A lifetime of witnessing the love and concern that other people show to those around them is a perfect preparation for understanding the goodness of life.

The middle age plus years give us more time to observe and experience and learn from these sermons. But this is really not about learning, but about feeling.

And I am getting a warm fuzzy feeling just telling each of you about these wonderful friends who have enriched my life.

MANY THINGS DIVIDE US

I enjoy making new friends. This week I made another new friend. She had known who I was, but I didn't know her. When I met her, I realized she looked very familiar, but I really didn't know who she was. She contacted me because of an article I wrote in the paper that mentioned that I have an old copy of the *Nevada Herald* that tells about the house she now owns. She wanted to see the paper and get a copy for her own history. We had a nice talk over the phone, and then she said she would come meet me in church the following Sunday. You see, this new friend attends the same church that we do, and we are often in the same service. But the problem is, she sits on the north side of the middle aisle. And what's more, she sits near the back, while we sit on the south side of the aisle, about in the middle. It's hard to believe that in a town as small as Nevada, in a church that is not huge, people do not know each other because they sit on the opposite sides of an aisle.

I do have some very good friends who sit on the north side of the church, and some of them even sit near the back. But I got acquainted with them some other way than by attending regular worship services together. My new friend said that once in a great while she does sit on *our* side of the aisle, but she just isn't comfortable. I understand. One time I needed to sit on the other side of the aisle because of a responsibility I had to greet a new-comer. I did it, but I felt like I was the visitor.

My new friend's cousin sits right behind us on our side but that had not made us get acquainted until the article in the paper brought us together. Sometimes when people go forward for communion, I try to pay attention to those neighbors on the north to get better acquainted, but it is hard to find out who everybody is.

This has made me think about other things that divide us. It used to be that people could live on the wrong side of the tracks and therefore not associate with the rest of the townspeople. That has changed quite a bit in recent years. In fact, in some communities the new subdivisions are sometimes created in what was formerly a *bad neighborhood.*

Rivers used to divide communities from each other. There are still some places where residents can see the buildings of others' farms but to drive there would take several miles of travel.

We live west of Nevada, which puts us only ten miles from the Kansas border. It wouldn't be far to visit folk in Bourbon County, but until Lester served an inter-im term as minister in that area, we didn't even know any of our western neighbors. However, we knew many people who lived that far away in eastern Vernon County or in other counties north, east, and south of us. Somehow that state line was a bigger division than county lines.

I worked in the election recently and as we watched people have to choose a certain party to get their ballot, I realized that politics also divide us somewhat. Many people didn't really care what the name of the party was—they just wanted to be able to vote for a certain person. They searched the lists to see which ballot gave them the opportunity to make that important vote.

Now that I am middle age plus, I begin to realize more that age sometimes divides us. The young whippersnappers don't want to associate with us old codgers as much as they prefer being with their own age group. We accentuate this by clubs designed for certain ages, regulations that require certain ages to qualify, and even newspaper page title, such as the "Senior Page."

I could get into more controversial divisions, such as sex, ethnic origins, sexual preference, marriage vs. significant others, or even bodily size. But many serious books are written on those subjects and need more research than I care to do right now. Which brings up another division—perfectionists or lazy slobs.

As an older, south of the aisle, married, overweight, tall, white woman, with children, grandchildren, and great-grandchildren, I will admit to falling into the category of a lazy slob. But just as some of the people across the aisle are good friends, some perfectionists also are counted as friends. It might just take a little more work to be sure that we don't get divided over that issue.

So let's tear down some of the walls that divide us— or at least cross over the imaginary lines we draw. I think the world will be a better place if we do. But don't look for me on the north side of our church. I like it where I am.

KEEP AN EYE ON SUSPICIOUS-LOOKING LITTLE OLD LADIES!

We all know the story about old dogs and new tricks. I don't like to compare myself to an old dog, but whatever I am, I learned a few new tricks over this last weekend as I traveled back to Connecticut to attend my sister Kathryn's memorial service.

The first trick was at the Kansas City International Airport where Lester took me to fly to Philadelphia to our son's home. I have flown many times and knew the ropes well. I walked up to the counter to get my boarding pass where I was told that I had an E ticket and didn't need to come to the counter but just to a machine nearby. Now I have gotten used to buying gas without going inside to pay for it, but this was new to me. I was instructed to push any old credit card in a slot and my boarding pass would come out. It didn't even have to be the credit card I used to pay for the ticket. A design came on the screen asking if I was checking luggage and giving me the choice of seats inside the plane. I got a seat on the first row behind first class, by the window, then my pass came through the slot and I was ready to fly.

Or almost ready to fly! There were several others in line putting their suitcases and purses on the traveling belt through the screening machine. They then were directed over to the waiting room seats. I blithely put my carry-on bag and purse on the belt and started through the arched doorway. Nothing whistled. No alarm went off. I was starting to follow the other passengers to the waiting room when I was pulled over and asked to take a seat.

While sitting there, I was asked to take off my shoes. The shoes were rather new and to make them more comfortable for travel, I had bought some cheap plastic innersole cushions and a lift for the heel because the tops of the shoe hit my ankle in an uncomfortable way without some padding. Of course, all these makeshift adjustments scattered when I took off my shoes. They were all put in the plastic pan and run through the machine again. I guess they thought anyone with that much extra stuff in her shoes must have been concealing something. And besides, I do look quite threatening!

The next step was worse. I was wearing my cherry-red weekender suit with a sleeveless turtleneck blouse under the jacket. I was instructed to stand (in my stocking feet—thank heavens I didn't have any holes in my socks!) on two painted footprints wide apart, take off my jacket (which was also run through the machine) and hold my arms out on each side. They whisked a screening device up and down every limb. The trouble was, there is a reason I wear jackets and/or long sleeves. My underarms are not one of my best features. There I stood with those bare arms revealing my sagging flesh, trying to look like a professional newspaper columnist, when they brought back the pan of materials I had stashed in my shoes and sat it down beside me. It was like putting a neon sign up saying, "Everyone look here at this old lady with the weird shoes." As soon as I passed muster, I found a chair and buried my nose in a book to show anyone who was watching that at least I could read.

The rest of the trip went well. My son and daughter-in-law met me and we drove in to Connecticut the next day to meet with family and attend the services on Saturday.

I planned ahead for the trip home, although I thought the chances of being picked on the second time were surely slim. Instead of wearing the sleeveless blouse under my suit, I wore a long sleeved turtleneck blouse. I rearranged the paddings in my shoes so that at least they all stayed together when the shoes were removed. I thought I was going to be fine even if they chose me again. I also checked my luggage so I wouldn't have as much to handle as I went through the lines.

Though the lines were much longer in the hub airport in Philadelphia, I advanced in line rather quickly and again watched most of those in front of me pass through security with no problem. But when I got there, they pulled me aside to the chairs. I went through the whole process again. This time I carried it off with aplomb. After all I am a seasoned traveler—even if I look suspicious to the guards. Do you think maybe older women wearing turtleneck blouses are targeted suspects? On my next trip, I will be driving. I will be more in control and that is the way I like it.

One of the worst things about these new experiences was that I couldn't tell Kathryn all about them. She would have had a good laugh with me about it all. That would have made it worthwhile. Maybe you can laugh with me instead?

DO YOU SMELL SOMETHING?

Do you smell something? What does it make you think of? I have found that I can bring back a memory of the past quicker when I detect a certain odor then any other way.

When I walk into an empty rural church, I am greeted with the comforting scent of musty hymnals, fragrance of past flower arrangements, mice droppings, and oiled floors. It makes me feel a part of a long meaningful history. The modern, larger church also has a distinctive odor of snuffed out candles, floral displays, remaining scent of perfume from the congregation members, and maybe a crushed crayon or dropped piece of chewing gum from one of the younger members.

For years the smell of a spirea bush gave me an image of a big red brick house with a chain and a hitching post out in front. I could feel that I was sitting on the concrete sides of the steps that led to this house. I didn't know what caused this memory until I described it to an aunt one day. She said that my grandmother's house fit this description and large spirea bushes surrounded it. Since my grandmother died when I was quite small, my nose had remembered more than my brain.

When I was a child, we used to identify the homes of our friends by distinct odors they had—not smells, just distinct odors. Some homes would have the aroma of cigar, pipe, or cigarette smoke to greet you as you entered. Others always smelled like fresh-baked bread or pies and jellies.

I wonder what odor others notice when they enter my home. Probably they will notice a burned smell because there has always been something spilled in the oven recently that continues to let its presence be known for several days each time the oven is lit. By the time it gets burned out—or I get it cleaned—another pie has spilled over or another baking potato has burst.

They may also notice the odor of newspapers and books. (If you don't believe they have an odor, go to the public library and you'll notice instantly that the printed page does have a scent.)

In the summer there is apt to be the smell of wetness because there is constantly a wet towel or bathing suit dropped on the bathroom floor.

I love the faint odor of sulfur that can be noticed near the waterworks in Nevada. Others cannot tolerate the smell at all, but for me it has meant I was getting near home. What is unpleasant for one can be a special odor for another.

My favorite *smelly story* is about a small girl who dearly loved an uncle who was a dairy farmer who fed silage to his cows daily. On a ride through the country, the family passed a farm where the odor of silage was particularly strong. The adults started to roll up their windows against the smell, but the child said, "Oh, doesn't that smell good? That smells just like Herbert."

Smells, like beauty, are in the eyes (or nose) of the beholder.

AULD LANG SYNE

How do you celebrate the New Year? Many people go to bed and let the New Year come in with no greeting at all. Others celebrate to the extent that they cannot drive home in the early hours of the next year. Most of us are in between there somewhere. New Year's Eve has often been a bit of a disappointment to me.

I remember the first time I stayed up for the event. That was before the days of television when my sister Ellen and I sat up in our living room and listened to the radio as they broadcast from a hotel ballroom. When midnight came, we ran out on our front porch and heard a few distant gunshots or firecrackers and then went back inside and listened to Tommy Dorsey's band playing "Auld Lang Syne." Somehow it didn't seem worth staying up for. We went to bed very soon, feeling that somehow we had missed the significance of it all.

A few years later I began to get to the dating age. Notice I said dating *age*, not when I began dating. Somehow when I became old enough for dates, it seemed no boys noticed that I was old enough. I knew I would be a dedicated old maid for sure. However, one year a girlfriend gave a party at which the girls were supposed to ask the boys. I got up my nerve and invited a boy. Fremont Hodson was his name. (I wonder whatever became of him.) He shocked me by accepting my invitation. The party was a complete disaster, not only for me but also for all who attended. I suspect that most of the group were on their very first date and first New Year's Eve party. We all sat around half the evening looking at each other. My friend's energetic mother didn't help matters with her tactless remarks such as, "A good-looking boy as you surely wants to dance with this lovely little girl," and so on.

Toward midnight when the boys began to run outside and throw snowballs at each other, the mother finally got us involved in a conga line which was to wind out the door and onto the sidewalk where we could shout our greetings at twelve to the world of 1942.

In the old movies, conga lines are carefree, hilarious lines of glamorous people gracefully winding through palms, flowers, and tables filled with exotic foods. However, in a girlfriend's living room with six awkward teenage couples, it lacked a little of the grace of an MGM spectacular. I tripped over the doorstep as we left the house on the stroke of midnight and greeted that New Year by sprawling into my date and knocking him to his knees. Somehow the rest of that year in school, we never did seem to find much to say to each other.

In college I often spent New Year's Eve on the train returning to the University of Missouri from my Christmas vacations with my family in Washington, D.C. I was usually miserable for one of two reasons: either some drunk had focused his attention on me and I sat huddled in a heap near the window hoping he wouldn't make a scene, or no one noticed me and I spent the evening in a heap near the window for fear someone would notice that no one noticed me!

In my married life we have celebrated the holiday with various other couples, family members, church youth groups, and in watch-night services. We found many different traditions for celebration, including eating salad at midnight, kissing your true love, and eating black-eyed peas. But most of the people we celebrated with didn't know how to handle such a momentous occasion any better than my teenaged friends did.

Someday I may find something really exciting to do to make a great occasion out of the celebration. But in these middle age plus years, I find it thrilling to just be breathing as another year rolls around.

I THINK I AM LEARNING TO LIKE SPIDERS

I have never liked snakes. I am not really afraid of them, and I can see them out in the wild without running in terror. However, I want them to stay out in the wild. I do not like snakes to invade *my* space. Of course, in the snake's view I am invading *its* space.

I have had several memorable occasions when I had too close an encounter with a snake to feel good about it. I have never actually killed a snake myself, but my pleas have caused some of the men in my life to kill one that was in a spot where I did not want to see it. One time my sister and I *worried* one to death when our mother wanted us to kill a big black snake that insisted on being across our back step. We anchored the poor thing down with a rock on each end so it could not get away, but neither of us could get up the nerve to actually wield the hoe to end its life. While we were trying to get up our courage, it seemed to lose its zest for life and died. We may have injured it with our rocks or maybe it was dying anyway. But somehow its life ended without either of us whacking it.

I grew up with a mother who was very afraid of snakes. She didn't even want to look at pictures of them.

We had an encyclopedia set that had a natural history volume with several full color pictures of various tropical snakes. When we teased her by showing her these pictures, she never really looked at them. However, she got a good look at one in our basement one summer. I can still hear her screams in my memory.

She was cleaning out a wash basin in the basement after a winter's accumulation of dust and wasps nests that gathered during the months we were in Washington. She pulled out a long white cord that was stuck in the drain, only to discover to her horror that it was a snake. Frozen with fear, she stood there holding the squirming reptile, yelling for our brothers to come rescue her. She either didn't want to let it go for fear it would get away . . . or fear of where it would go if she dropped it. So she just held it until the boys reached her side. They disposed of it quickly. We still don't know if it was an albino black snake, or if it had lived in the drain all its life and therefore had no color. But it was big, long, healthy, and undoubtedly quite shocked by the episode.

I have never enjoyed going down into that basement since then. When our sister Miriam lived there, she was glad to have some black snakes living in the basement. She said they caught the mice. She even named one she often saw. I never got that close.

In our first parsonage at Archie, our little house had a closet in each bedroom and a wrap closet in the living room. I had spent the morning cleaning out the closet in our sons' room, carrying out all sorts of icky stuff and trash. When the job was over, I opened the closet door in the living room to get a jacket, and there on the nice clean floor was a huge black snake. I yelled at the kids to stay in their rooms and pulled the phone into my bedroom to call Lester to come home from the church to kill one of God's creatures. He couldn't come right away and told me there was nothing to be afraid of. In the meantime Michael, disobeying my orders to stay in his room, jumped over the snake, which by now was out in the living room, and ran for a hoe to carry it outside to kill it.

When Lester returned, I asked how on earth a snake that large could get in our house. He told me that a snake could go anywhere a mouse could. That was little comfort, for in spite of some house cats, we did have trouble with mice in that house. That night when I went into the boys' room to tell them goodnight, I nearly jumped out of skin, yelling at what I saw on the floor. The boys had arranged their belts and socks on the floor in a curved pattern that in the dim light from the hall looked like a snake. They still laugh at this memory. I finally reached the point where I can at least smile about it.

I had some childhood scares with snakes when I was in the barefoot stage. Once I jumped on a stick across the sidewalk and it slithered away. Another time I was trapped in the outhouse by a snake that had come to sun itself in the half-opened door while I was browsing through the Sears Roebuck catalog. Since no one answered my calls for help, I gathered my courage, jumped over the snake, and broke a speed record back to the house.

Now, why am I telling all these snake stories to you now?

Recently, I was beginning to do a little cleaning in the closed-in east porch of our house. When I noticed that the cobwebs were pretty thick in a few places, I started to clear some out. A small bent twig was in one cobweb near the front door. For some reason I took a second look at the twig and realized it had a tiny head and a curved tail. A very small, thin snake was caught up in the web and seemed to be dead. It wasn't more than eight inches long and was not as wide as a ballpoint pen. But it was definitely a snake.

I may never clean house again. Or at least I will leave all spider webs alone.

I WILL BE WALKING MY BODY BACK HOME

I was watching the *Today Show* recently when a guest on the show talked about how little effort it took to lose weight and keep in shape. He said just walking one and a half miles a day for one year will cause you to lose fourteen pounds regardless of what other changes you might make in your lifestyle.

I thought, *That sounds easy. I like to walk. I'll start doing that.* So, on Monday I charted out what I thought a mile and a half would be. You would think that living in the country would make this very simple. It would . . . except for five things—neighbors' dogs. If I go out our driveway and turn south so that I could walk to various friends' homes, I have to pass two houses where the dogs join together to make a formidable obstacle to pass on the road, especially for someone who is alone.

I am not afraid of dogs really. Some of my best friends have been dogs. But when a *gang* of five dogs runs together, I do get a bit intimidated. I suppose I could walk softly and carry a big stick, but that would probably be a challenge for the dogs to accept.

So I must plan a route that doesn't turn south at our mailbox. The next option would be to go north, but there

is no good turnaround that way and just going three quar-
ters of a mile one way and turning around and coming
back sounds rather dull. Besides, if I pass my granddaughter's house, the great-grandchildren will want to go
with me. That would defeat the purpose of a nice brisk
walk. That type of walk comes later.

I decided to do my walking on our own property and
use the exercise time as a chance to commune with nature
and check on things on the farm. I figured if I went north
to the edge of our lawn, then west to the edge of the field,
turned south to meet the driveway of our family home,
went west to go around the granary, circled the pond
twice, and returned to our home, I would have the
required distance. Much of this distance will be in thick
grass, but at this time of the year, there are no weeds (or
chiggers) to contend with. I figured I made a pleasant
choice of my route.

Walking has worked out very well so far. On days
when my daughter is not working, I might persuade her
to join me on part of the tour. The views are relaxing and
even in this bleak time of winter, the views are quite
pleasant.

Yesterday, since Lester needed to go to town, I decided to vary my route by riding with him to the highway
and walking back home. I knew that was exactly one and
a half miles, and I could time myself. Then when I chose
still other routes, I could judge by the time I was taking
when I was getting enough distance.

This was an excellent choice. There was no thick
grass to contend with, and I didn't have to watch my feet
as much since the gravel on the road is well packed down
this time of year. I was free to look around and enjoy the
scenes around me. I heard one car coming and knew it
was my daughter going to work. She would understand

why I was walking out on the road. Two small vans passed me right behind each other. The drivers each waved at me but didn't stop to ask questions.

When I passed our good neighbor's home, he stepped out on the porch to see if I needed a ride somewhere. I explained I was out for exercise. We waved. I realized he might have noticed me passing with Lester in the pickup earlier and may have thought we had car trouble and I was walking for help, or maybe that we had had a fight and I was going home in a huff. Whatever he might have thought, I straightened him out and went on, thinking how nice it is to have good neighbors.

As I passed our granddaughter's house, her little dog joined me so I had company for a while. When I reached home I felt very pleased with myself. For five days I had kept to my plan. I enjoyed the pleasure of neighbors, daughters, granddogs, nature, and wind in my face. I hadn't cheated myself once nor have I cut corners.

So I began to bring up my math skills from college. If I could lose 14 pounds in 365 days, how many pounds had I lost in these five days? Let's see, I think it goes 365 is to 14 what x is to 5. Or is it, 365 is to 5 what x is to 14? I'm quite sure it isn't 365 is to x as 14 is to 5. That doesn't make good sense. Maybe another way to figure would be that 5 is what percent of 365 and take that percent of 14. Or I guess I could just weigh myself.

I am getting good exercise but now I know I need to exercise this middle age plus brain a bit too. I shouldn't forget my algebra after only fifty-seven years. What good is an education if you can't remember how to use it?

Anyway, when you see me the next time, be prepared to see just a shadow of my former self. I will lose these pounds either in our fields or on the road, but no one needs to bring them back to me.

WHAT WE HAVE HERE
IS A SURPLUS
OF COMMUNICATION

Because of all the timesaving communication equipment we have in our home, I almost didn't have time to do my daily writing today. I started the day out early this morning with an idea of what I was going to write. Before I even started, I got a telephone call from Shirley wanting me to test her new cell phone by calling so she could see what it sounded like. I did, but it sounded like nothing. So I had to use our regular phone to call her regular phone to tell her I tried, but nothing happened. Two or three trials later I discovered that I was dialing the wrong number. That does make a difference. Even this high tech instrument can't read my mind like the old Central operators could. If I didn't have someone's number, then she could not only give me the right number but could tell me that the person I was calling was in town this morning.

Anyway, we got Shirley's cell phone to ring and she now knows what to listen for. That reminded Lester that he had stopped by the cell phone store in town to see about adding a phone for him onto my contract with the company. He brought all the material for me to look at so we could make a decision on whether we wanted to try that plan. It would be very handy when he is out on the tractor and I need to contact him. But could he even hear it over the sound of the tractor? Since being middle age plus does diminish our hearing somewhat, I don't know if the little ding-ding the phones have would alert him to a call. We decided to sleep on that decision.

Next, I got a phone call from my grandson, giving me the numbers of motels near his home in Illinois. His wife is graduating from college on May 4 and is due to give birth to our sixth great-grandchild around April 4, so they are celebrating both events on May 4. Naturally, since many of her family will be coming as well as our carload, we need to make motel reservations. When Kevin said they were filling up fast due to the graduation, I decided I should hurry to do so.

First I had to check with my sister to see if she would like to join us on the trip. I turned to my email to contact her. There were seven messages, two of which were from the same sister, so I had to read all of them before sending my message.

One of the messages was an important bit of information that I needed to act upon right away, so before I emailed Ellen, I answered the other message. Thankfully, since Ellen had her computer on, I got her answer quickly and was able to make my call to reserve some beds for us in Illinois.

The 800 number for the motel answered quickly. I got my reservations made with no problem. That is, with no problem until the nice lady on the other end said, "Oh, oh!" Her computer screen went blank, and she lost all the information she had already gathered from me. I had put my credit card back in the slot in my bill-fold, zipped the billfold shut, put it in my purse, and zipped the purse shut. I had to get it out again to give her all the information the second time. Then she asked if I was interested in a discount I could get for the cost of the rooms. Of course I was, but that hooked me up with a computerized voice that rattled on and on about all the goodies I could get with a program they could offer. I didn't want to hang up for fear I would mess up my reservation information again. I listened through the long patter and made my decision.

So now I could return to my writing. Being pretty thirsty from all the talking and listening, I went to get a drink and passed the telephone answering machine. You guessed it . . . it was blinking its little heart out with seven messages that I had not noticed when I returned home last night. One of them needed an answer right away. I had to search out a piece of paper and pencil to jot down the information from the other six. Since I couldn't hear one message clearly enough to get the return number I had been given, I had to replay the entire list of messages two more times. I think there is a way to get to the message you want to hear without going through the whole thing, but I don't know how. Not wanting to risk losing the information on the messages, I heard the whole thing for the third time.

Now, back to my computer to write. In my frustration, I have forgotten my original subject. I will use this marvelous communication tool, and then I will get back to the messages on the answering machine. If any of you readers left those messages, be patient with me. I'll get back to you just as soon as I can because your call is important to me. But first I have to find Lester to tell him about another call that just came. I wonder if I could just buy a big dinner bell somewhere. Or maybe try smoke signals?

TIME TO COME OUT OF THE CLOSET

Now that cold weather has really arrived, I thought it was time for me to put my summer things in the spare room closet and bring out all my winter clothes. It's not like I have to pull down the attic stairs as I did at the parsonage in Archie or go down in the basement to make this change. The two rooms are side by side, and I can easily get clothes from one to another. But as the cold weather began to appear and holiday garb was in style, I was gradually bringing winter things into my closet without taking the summer things out. Naturally this made a nice cozy closet with wrinkled clothes and tangled hangers.

I also decided that this was a good time to clean out my closet and get rid of those clothes I haven't worn for several years. Some I haven't worn because I didn't really like them very well. Others were put in the back because they had shrunk through the years so that they no longer fit me. The humidity has gotten worse in our house as I have reached middle age plus. I can tell because my clothes shrink while they are hanging on the hangers. That didn't happen as much when I was younger.

I began pulling out some of the seldom-seen clothes from the back and discovered several garments I had forgotten all about. A Christmas shirt I bought toward the end of the season a couple years ago got pushed back in with some of the shrunken clothes. It is perfectly good and didn't get too small. I can't discard that one.

Another pair of slacks seemed a little tight but when I put them on, I realized if I always wore them with an overblouse or sweater the tightness wouldn't show. I put them back where I found them.

I unearthed a very nice dress that I hadn't worn but once or twice because I felt too dressed up in it. But I never know when there will be an occasion when being very dressed up is what is needed. It rejoined its friends in the closet also.

I must have a dozen tee shirts or sweatshirts proclaiming organizations I have worked for, belonged to, or supported. Naturally I couldn't give any of them away even if I couldn't possibly wear all of them in any one season.

There are two pairs of jeans I wear almost every day of the week. The new stretch ones I wear when I go to town. The older ones with the elastic top I wear around home. Actually with those two pairs and maybe a pair of dressy slacks, I would have all I actually need. But it is hard to part with some of these friends that have hung around so long.

I did find a cotton shirtwaist dress that went to the pile of giveaways. And there were a couple of jackets that pulled across my shoulders when I wore them. I didn't want to risk having my clothes tear off me while I was out in public. I put them in the pile. I couldn't part with the dress I wore to Shirley's wedding or the junior bridesmaid dress twelve-year-old Susan wore. Mark's cap and gown from high school graduation remained snugly among the souvenir clothing as did the long skirt I had to wear to a Christmas party once about twenty years ago. Maybe someday when my heirs go through my things after I am gone, one of them will cherish these garments—even if there's no way to figure out what they were for.

I hesitated to get started on evaluating the coats and jackets in the wrap closet. But I decided I'd better do a complete job while I was at it. There is a wonderful cape that I bought at Levy's in Butler at least thirty years ago. It is perfectly good and very warm. Of course, I never wear it because it is awkward to wear while driving. I found my favorite sweater-coat hiding among the heavier ones and decided it would have a renaissance this year. I would really wear it again. Everything else was what I am still wearing or too worn to give away, yet too good to throw away. My giveaway pile didn't get any bigger from that closet. Nor did the closet get any roomier.

I reviewed my morning's work. I had five garments to donate somewhere. I found $1.28 in the pockets of some of the winter clothing I brought out. I got reacquainted with some very nice clothes. And I decided that I was well supplied with clothes for many more seasons. Of course, that depends on whether we can lick the humidity problem. I still need to have clothes to wear to church, but not nearly as many as when Lester was the minister. A retired minister's wife can look dumpy and no one will care. Clothing needs are quite different for me now.

I felt guilty that I wasn't either throwing away or giving away more of my things. Then I realized what I really needed to thrown away. I took all the clothing sales catalogs from the magazine rack and put them in the recycling pile. That was what I had too much of.

Now my two closets have the proper clothes for the season on the racks. But they are still crowded and it won't be long before the hangers get tangled again.

Maybe next week I will start organizing the drawers of my dressers. Or I could wait until spring.

TIME AND TIDE WAIT FOR NO ONE

I work well under pressure. When I have a deadline facing me, I can usually get things done in a hurry. If I find out I am having unexpected company coming, I can usually do a quick make over of the living room before the guests are out of their car. Making preparations for a meeting, a speech, or even writing an essay can usually be done in a very short time—if I am against a deadline. It is the jobs that I plan to do *someday* that take so long to do. Jobs that I should do while I have more time but with the deadline still a day or two away also get put off. Those are the duties I procrastinate about.

When I sit down to write and there are still a few days left before anyone needs to have my copy, I can think of all sorts of things to do first. For one thing, whenever I turn on the computer I have to check my Free Cell average on my favorite computer game. If it is below fifty percent then it is obvious that I need to play a few games to bring it up to a respectable score. That is when the computer game demon gets to me. I think they have it rigged so that the first game or two you play gets solved easily. You feel so good about your abilities that you plan to play just one more game to pad that average a bit. Then the demon takes over. All the aces are in a different line and clear at the top. At the bottom of the line are all the kings and queens. It doesn't take long to lose that game. Though it doesn't matter too much because you have already brought your average up a bit, you think it would be better to play one more game to even out the loss. Then two more to even out both loses. Soon the spare time you had to write is gone. Now you feel too frustrated to be creative anymore anyway.

Another way that time gets used up is trying to listen to a TV program and do a job at the same time. I used to watch my children do their homework on the floor in front of the TV. They seemed to do okay, both with the TV plot and their grades. I know this isn't a preferred method, but they seemed to do well with it. The programs must be getting more detailed, or I am not as swift as my children were. I soon get lost in the programs and either mess up the job I am doing or forget about working on the job at all. Age couldn't have anything to do with this, could it?

One of my biggest distractions is the view from our house. There is always something that I should watch outside. It wouldn't be right to ignore all the gifts of nature I can see and just keep my eyes glued to a square computer monitor. Right now the geese are vying for territory in our pond. I have to watch to be sure that our pair is the one that wins the nest box. To be sure it is *our* pair, I must go outside with a handful of corn and speak to the birds. If it is the ones who have claimed us as their benefactors, they will come toward me and wait for me to toss the tidbits of corn to them. If it is a different pair, they will swim or fly away as soon as I open the door toward the pond.

Now we have an acrobatic squirrel that has adopted us also. (I think there really are two, but we only see one at a time.) Watching him find ways to get feed from the bird feeders is amusing. The grace and agility of this little animal is amazing. I gladly share bird food with him to have the opportunity to watch his actions.

Other birds, the waves on the pond in this windy March weather, the movement of the clouds in a blue sky—all these things need to be looked at daily or I will feel ungrateful for this beautiful world we live in. Then that reminds me that the plants I have brought inside for the winter probably need watering. One of the cats will rouse from her nap when I start moving around and decide she needs some TLC. She will plop on her back in front of me as I walk, turning her tummy up to be scratched. That action cannot be denied, so I oblige her request, which brings another cat to get the same treatment.

I don't know what has happened to the time but suddenly it is getting dark. I haven't even thought about what I would have for supper and I haven't started writing.

I said I work well under pressure, so I now am under pressure to get something on the table to eat for supper. I will do that just as soon as I check to see if there is a new moon in the darkening sky. And while I am at it, I will see what the temperature reads on the outside thermometer. I want to keep track of these things to compare from year to year. However, I forget to write the data down when I get back inside and can't remember it even to the next day.

Back to supper—I just remembered Lester has a meeting tonight. We'd better eat real soon. What can I get ready in time? Thank heavens for microwaves!

MUM'S THE WORD WHEN YOU WHISPER A MESSAGE

One of the joys of having children, grandchildren, or great-grandchildren is that they like to share things with their elders. I recently spent parts of three days baby-sitting my two and a half-year-old great-granddaughter. We had a nice time, but we went through a box of Kleenex quickly because Michaella had a bad cold. In spite of frequent hand washings (both hers and mine), I came down with her cold last Thursday. At first it was just a bit of hoarseness and a runny nose. Then the next day it was quite a bit of hoarseness and still a drippy nose. On Saturday I was one of five women putting on a writing workshop at Cottey College, and because I was the local presenter, I was acting as host and coordinator.

I awoke that morning barely able to whisper. Some orange juice, other liquids, and willpower got me going where I was at least croaking enough to be heard. By nursing a Dr. Pepper throughout the day to keep my throat moist and my energy up and by drafting Shirley to do most of the readings I was scheduled to do, I made it through the day. I'm not sure any of the participants heard anything I said, but that probably was okay. They heard the other four who are more experienced than I anyway.

I was scheduled to teach a Sunday School class on Sunday. Lester decided that the class wouldn't want to hear my raspy voice so he called our friend, Leonard, to fill in for me. It was a good thing because by Sunday morning I not only could not talk above a whisper, I was coughing my head off. No one wants to sit in church with someone who is alternating between coughing and blowing her nose. So I stayed home and even took a little nap. That made me mad. I thought that I so seldom was at home on Sunday mornings that this would be a good chance to see what we were missing on television. I still don't know because I slept through it.

Monday didn't bring a lot of relief in the voice part, but since I was coughing up a lot of yucky stuff, I consoled myself that I was getting better. By the time you read this if my name hasn't been in the obits, then you can assume I am all well again.

This fascinating account of my ailment has caused me to notice a lot of things about such maladies.

Why is it that when someone can't talk, all anyone else can seem to do is ask questions? Sometimes they don't even look at you when you try to answer. In that case sign language is of no use.

A similar thing happens also. Since I was not talking, the others in any group I was in also fell silent. Long pauses with no conversations occurred until someone realized what was happening and came up with—you guessed it—a question.

Since my voice was very, very low due to my cold, those who were talking to me seemed to also lower their voices. I do have some hearing difficulties but not enough to make me miss all the quiet words I was hearing directed my way.

Don't think I am picking on my poor husband. Actually, he wasn't the culprit in this situation. He even brought me a Butterfinger Blizzard. That sounded like it would go down easily. It did.

Telephone conversations were fun. People who knew of my problem would then try to cut the conversation short. Others who called were not sure they had made connections or thought their cell phone was acting up. On the phone you can't even use nods of your head or finger pointing.

I know there are many people who go through life not able to speak. These three days of silence have convinced me that I would not do well in such a condition. I constantly thought of things I wanted to tell any and everyone. Even when I was watching TV, I found I wanted to comment on the plot. Over the sounds of the program no one could hear me, but I persisted anyway.

Every morning I go outside to give a little corn to the gander that is patrolling the pond while his lady is sitting on the nest. I usually wish him a good morning and ask how the goose is getting along. Today, without speaking, I went outside and threw the corn. He looked at me for a long time before he began to eat. I guess he wanted to be sure I was still his friend.

The cats haven't noticed my silence as long as I pet them occasionally. And the great-granddaughter who shared the malady with me in the first place is again hale and hearty and hasn't been around to notice my symptoms. I think being middle age plus made mine a little different from hers. I can't get away with being cranky and cross. I'm a big girl now and can even blow my own nose.

ORGANIZING EXPERIENCES ARE NOT ALWAYS PLEASANT

One of the keys to a successful marriage is to do any rearranging of your personal space when your spouse is out of town. Lester and I have home offices where we each have our computers, desks, and files. Maybe it is the weather, or maybe it is the beginning of the school year, but for some reason, unplanned by the other, we each decided to do some rearranging of our separate work areas.

My plan was to get a handy little tall, narrow file cabinet to stick between my computer desk and the kneehole desk to store the papers that accumulate. Since I didn't find just what I wanted on my first shopping expedition, I bought some stand-up files instead. I splurged on some nice brightly colored file folders to replace the tired old manila folders I have been using for years. I had turned them inside out and pasted labels over the notations so many times that the little tabs had lost all their starch. I pictured the bright colors cluing me to the contents of each folder before I looked at the notations.

When I began my reorganization, it was soon apparent that I needed something more. I returned to the store and found the file I was looking for in the laundry department. The cases are designed to fit between a washer and a dryer.

Back home again I filled a wastebasket with old material. Some of it dated back thirty years. I loaded the colored files and eventually got all of the papers off of the floor and organized neatly. I saw the top of my computer desk for the first time in weeks.

In the meantime Lester decided to move his office to a different location. Since he was leaving some materials in the former spot, he now had room for some extra shelves. A set of shelves had been in our bedroom for several years, accumulating things that you put on shelves when you are not quite sure where you want to put them. This looked to be the right size for what he needed. But that meant finding a home for all the things that had been living on these shelves. The obvious spot was to pile them on the bed until the shelves got moved.

But wait a minute. The best spot for the shelves was where the extra refrigerator sits in the breezeway. That is no problem. We will move the old refrigerator out to the enclosed back porch where we keep all the stuff that will be recycled eventually. Of course, to do that we had to find a place to put all the aluminum cans, the sacks of newspapers, cardboard boxes, and metal cans. It will be several days until the recycling center will be open again, so we moved most of those articles outside the back door.

Using a dolly to move the appliance made that job fairly easy—until a high step at the back door was too high. We didn't want to take too long on this because the things we use this refrigerator for are mainly frozen goods and the nearly ninety degree weather didn't allow much time before the stuff would thaw. Using brute force, some encouraging words, and ramps of concrete blocks, two-by-fours, and other nearby materials, we finally got that problem settled and went back to positioning the shelves.

At this time I decided that my best bet would be to return to the bedroom and see if I could make it possible for us to go to bed sometime that night. Some of the things that had been on the now removed shelves were photograph albums and scrapbooks. I couldn't find a new home for them without looking through them again. This took some time and reminded me that one of my next jobs must be to get back to filing all my pictures so that future relatives will know whose face they are seeing. I was jolted by a picture of me holding one of my great-grandchildren who was about six months old. I couldn't tell if it was Shelbie or her little brother, Jerron, because the pictures had become so mixed up. Nothing was written on the back. I put those albums in a noticeable place so that I would not forget the job I needed to do very soon.

I found a temporary place for everything and tried to avoid looking outside our back door where it looked like we were starting the city dump. Before actually going to bed, I decided I would feel better if I went in to my own newly organized workspace.

I turned on the computer to check my email. A message on the machine required information from one of my new file folders. This was my first opportunity to test out my new system. My mind went blank—possibly some post-traumatic stress disorder from all the confusion of the day—but I could not remember where I had filed that information. I remembered it was in a red folder, probably one of the ones on top of my desk. I couldn't find it. I looked through all the red folders and still had no luck. As I was about to give up, I decided to try out the little narrow file cabinet and there, in a bright blue file, was the information I needed.

If a marriage can last fifty-seven years, maybe it will withstand rearranging our personal spaces. And we did get to go to bed that night.

MOVIE GOING BROUGHT UP TO DATE

When I was a little girl, one of my favorite things was to go to the movies. In Nevada, we drove in town to the Star Theater on Saturday afternoon to see whatever movie was showing. There were always cartoons, coming attractions, newsreels, and sometimes a special short subject. In the winter when we lived in Washington, D.C., we walked to the Avalon Theater on Saturday afternoons, or if we were lucky, we accompanied our parents for their usual Monday night *date* downtown to see a first-run movie on F Street. Two of the downtown theaters presented a *stage show* between the showings of the film. A remnant of the old time vaudeville, this part of the program also included featured actors.

One time I saw Ronald Reagan on stage when he was a "B" movie actor. Being a movie fan, I was very excited when we ate in the Willard Coffee Shop afterward and saw him eating at a nearby table. My father wouldn't let me ask for an autograph. If I had, I wonder what it would be worth today—if I had kept it and could find it.

At that time the first-run movies started out in the big cities on the two coasts and gradually worked their way inland to smaller towns. Sometimes the movies that we saw at the Star Theater in the summer were the ones we had already seen downtown in Washington before we came back to Vernon County. That didn't matter. We often saw the same movie several times—sometimes in one sitting.

As I got older and began dating, most often we would go to the movies and then get something to drink afterwards. During the war (WWII) many of the movies were about the war. They were romantic films about the girl that was waiting at home, meeting at the stage door canteen, USOs, or having a last night together in London before D-Day.

There were battle scenes also. I will always remember one scene, although I don't know what movie it was shown in. It was about a young soldier from the hills. He was in a foxhole talking to his buddy and had taken off his boots to air his feet. Shooting began and the country boy reached up to get his boots from the top of the foxhole, got hit with a bullet, and before he died, called out, "Mama." I was a teenager and could feel with the soldier the desperate need of a mother at such a time.

When Lester and I were dating at Columbia while in college, we often walked to the Missouri or Uptown Theaters. We never drove because of the gas shortage. The walk was part of the fun. I remember in one of the movies we saw together another poignant scene from a war movie that starred Van Johnson. It showed soldiers packed in a railroad car being sent overseas. One of them starting singing "Leaning on the Everlasting Arms." I cried.

When our children were little, if we lived in a town that had a theater, Lester and I took them to the movies. We always had to economize in those early days in the ministry with very low salaries. I remember sitting through Dr. Zhivago with four-year-old Susan in my lap. Though I was nearly paralyzed when the movie was over, holding her saved us from buying another ticket.

Now with all this history of movie going, why was it such an event that Lester and I went to see a movie last weekend? Because it had been years since we had done this. With the advent of television, VCR, and inflated ticket costs, we had fallen away from the habit. This was even the first time we had been in the new theater here in Nevada.

Our first problem was finding where the movie we wanted to see was being shown within the multiplex theater building. Since this was in the afternoon (cheaper tickets!) and there were many children there to see *Ice Age*, the movie personnel were too busy to notice our confusion.

The movie was *We Were Soldiers*. It was excellent in many ways. Since it was a true story, we were caught up in the reality of it. The realism was so graphic that some scenes were hard to watch. Unlike the earlier war movies, this one brought us right into the middle of the gory mess that is called war. There were still the emotions of the ones left behind at home, but the technicolor battle scenes ran red. The sound system that allowed us to hear the planes and helicopters, coming from the distance and passing by, added to the already graphic realism.

I am glad we went. I was impressed by the technology of the new theaters and the new movies. I was equally impressed by the real life soldiers who lived this story during the Vietnam War. But I was immensely saddened at the realization that after all this pain, death, and destruction, nothing was really settled, and we are still in a world that thinks war is the answer.

LIFE'S PARADOXES HIT AT ANY AGE

I keep finding many paradoxes in life these days. This week on the front cover of the FYI section of the *Kansas City Star* there was a long article, complete with a large picture, about teenaged boys and young adult men shaving their chests. I read the material while remembering that it wasn't long ago that a boy was proud to be able to show a few hairs on his chest. A popular saying was, "This'll grow hair on your chest," when referring to a wholesome drink or a challenging experience. Why would these young men want to add to their daily routines with one more cosmetic chore when men were created to have hairy chests? Then I looked down at my legs and realized women were being just as foolish.

To add to the paradox, on the bottom of the page was a picture of an Afghanistan woman refugee, nearly covered from head to foot, sitting on a crude bed in a tent. A newborn baby was lying behind her on the bed. The baby was covered with a coarse-looking blanket and seemed to be asleep. The contrast between worrying about unwanted hair on body parts and worrying about food, shelter, and a future for a child were vividly displayed on the same page.

In another section of the paper there was a segment on fashions for the younger adults. Many of the styles were loose and hung shapelessly from the shoulders of the models. The sizes seemed too large and bulky. However, again on the same page, were the styles that looked like someone had skimped on the material. The bottoms of the blouses did not meet the tops of the skirts or slacks. The neckline was wide and low and often the garment was sleeveless. Remembering the styles of the 1940s when the exact length of the hemline was a crucial point, I wondered how those who were concerned about such things knew which was the proper style. I guess the answer is that both styles are proper. The same person will one day appear in baggy, oversized slacks and top and the next day will be wearing the slightly enlarged bikinis. It reminded me of a remark my brother-in-law, Dudley, made to Kathryn when they were leaving for Sunday School with their four grade-school-aged children. He said, "Why is it that none of our kids ever have clothes that fit them right now? They are always growing out of them or growing into them." Today they would all be completely in style.

Another paradox has to do with time. Many of my middle age plus friends have retired. Part of the reason for their retirement was so they would have more time to do the things they would like to do. But most of them are now busier than they were when they were working. The churches and service organizations are grateful for this, but some retired people feel caught in a maze of activities. A common remark is "I don't know how I ever had time to work." Of course, they didn't get as involved in other activities, or perhaps they organized their days a little better, but the idle retired person is a rarity. In fact, the word retired might be changed to redirected. And it may also be that it takes us *slightly* longer to get each job done than it did before. Anyway you look at it, it is a paradox.

Other amusing contradictions have to do with budgeting. Living on a fixed income means we need to watch our pennies. So we drive all over town to get the bargain buys we see advertised in the paper. A gallon of gas here and there isn't much compared to the twenty-seven cents we can save. (Maybe this running around for bargains is part of the reason we don't have enough time for other things?)

I don't feel that I fit in that last category. I usually stick to one grocery store, one bank, one beauty shop, one drive-in, and certainly one church. I could be called a creature of habit, but it is nice to be known and to know what to expect when you enter the doors of a chosen establishment. So when stopping at my favorite grocery store this week, I entered to find the shopping baskets are no longer where they had been. The walls have been knocked out. Things are rearranged and I can't find the cheese sticks. I know the store is being improved, but my familiar style of shopping was completely upset—I didn't know which aisles to zip to in a hurry and didn't have my grocery list in the order the products were arranged in the store.

I laughed with the other shoppers as we played hide-and-seek with the personnel. They hid the food. We sought it. I knew the disruption would soon be over, and I would get used to the new arrangement. I comforted myself that at least this was the same familiar store, even with new arrangements, and I was a known and valued customer known by most of the staff. I finished my shopping and went to the checkout where I paid for my purchases with a check. The new employee looked at my check and said she would have to see some identification. So much for being known and valued!

The biggest paradox is that even in my mature years, I could become so annoyed at the situation that I protested the action and made the poor girl very uncomfortable. That cashier probably will know me in the future, but I am not sure I will be valued.

A DAILY HEALTH ROUTINE

When the world is in a crisis, we sometimes begin to feel like everything we do or say needs to be very meaningful, thought provoking, or inspirational. Thoughts about what we are going to have for supper or wondering if it is time to get a haircut seem rather trivial. But there is a limit to the time I can be serious and somber. I feel better if I can have a good laugh now and then.

I did some research on the Internet. (I wonder whatever happened to doing research in a book?) I found that if you laugh a hundred times a day, you have done as much good for your body as ten minutes on a rowing machine or an exercise bike. I couldn't find out how much good it would do for you to laugh for ten minutes while you are riding an exercise bike. That might overdo it since I also found out that laughter can lead to hiccuping and coughing and can clear out the respiratory track. But if you are middle age plus, such laughing, hiccuping, and coughing can lead to other problems not related to your respiratory track. So we take a breather and just smile for a while so that we keep our dignity. My teeth are still my own, but I have seen some people laugh so hard that they lost their false teeth. There are other ways we might lose our dignity also.

Did you know that you can't make yourself laugh by tickling yourself? Try it. I did and found that the facts are true. If someone else tickles the bottom of my feet, I can't help but laugh. When I do it to myself, it's ho-hum time.

I like to watch how people laugh. Okay, help me out now and laugh out loud. Was your laugh a ha ha, a ho ho, a heh heh, heh, a humpf, or a huh, huh, huh? I think I fit in the last category, but I can't really decide. Sometimes I think I do the real ha ha ha bit too.

My research tells me that laughter increases blood pressure, increases heart rate, changes breathing, reduces levels of neurochemicals, and provides a boost to the immune system. What's more, when we laugh, fifteen facial muscles contract and stimulation of the zygomatic major muscles occurs. I didn't make that name up to make you laugh. It is the lifting mechanism of your upper lip. What middle age plus person wouldn't like to have the upper lip stimulated? At least then we can know we still have these facial features.

I think I have decided what I will do these days to lift my spirits. I will find a hundred things to laugh at each day. Our new kitten should provide a few opportunities. The squirrel stealing birdseed, the flowers popping through the ground, and the sound of the birds returning usually bring my smiles. Now I will change those smiles to laughs.

There is still another bigger source of reasons to laugh. Each time my husband or I lose a paper that was just on the table and we haven't moved from our seat, I can laugh at us. When I go to the bedroom in a hurry to get something I need and then forget what it was that I needed, I will laugh. And when someone calls to try to sell me a set of children's books, I will be like Sarah in the Bible, and I will laugh.

I should be the healthiest person around.

PROGRESS IS WONDERFUL— ONCE YOU HAVE MASTERED IT

I wonder if my ancestors were reluctant to change from having a car that you had to crank to getting one with a starter. It seems a silly question now. Of course, it was better, easier, and quicker to have a starter that worked from inside the car than having to be outside in front of the car, breaking your back trying to crank the engine into starting. It is just as silly as the reluctance I have had at various times to change from a comfortable way of doing things to trying something new and different.

I felt there was no reason for me to learn to use a computer. I had a very nice electronic typewriter that did everything I thought I needed. In fact, it was with great reluctance that I changed from a manual typewriter to an electric one and then on to the electronic one. My earliest writing was done very easily with a pencil and a large tablet. I could do it anyplace I wanted to be. I could carry it with me and write a few lines while riding in the car or waiting for a family member to do an errand. The supplies were cheap, I needed no instructions, and all my energies were used in creating the words I was putting on the paper. Later, of course, I had to make these words more easily read by others, so I would copy from the tablet with a typewriter. I was happy with this arrangement.

Then I was persuaded it would save time if I had an electronic typewriter so that I could compose directly on the instrument and make corrections as I went with the wonderful abilities that machine had. My only problem was a lazy third finger on my right hand. As I was typing on these easily compressed keys, that finger would sometimes sag a bit and the letter "L" would appear in odd places in my composition. If I noticed it, I could take care of it immediately with the delete key, but I didn't always see the mistake until much later. However, I was happy with this arrangement.

All this time my husband, sister, and friends were entering the world of computers. Their frustrations as they were mastering this technology convinced me that in these middle age plus years there was no way that I would even try to join them in this computerized world. I wasn't in that big of a hurry. I could take a little more time and be relaxed in my comfortable way of doing things. So what if I occasionally had to retype a page or two. Sometimes I could spot a better way of expressing a thought and use that time to improve the text. No, I was not going to be tempted.

One day I had a technical problem with my electronic typewriter and needed to get my column into the paper. I reluctantly agreed to use Lester's computer just to get that column done. He was right by my side so that I didn't have the pressure of trying to figure out how to proceed. Well, maybe there was a little pressure when he had to tell me for the third time how to set my margin or indent my paragraphs. I'm not a slow learner. I just had to prove that using a computer was harder than anything I wanted to tackle.

Surprisingly, the column turned out fine and when I found the cost of fixing the electronic typewriter, I decided that maybe it would be okay to get a computer—just to use it as I would use a typewriter.

Then I found the joys of email. I began corresponding with people I usually only sent Christmas cards to. I would send and receive three or four messages from the same person the same day. It was almost like talking on the phone, only I couldn't hear their voices. But I did have a written record of what was said, so I wouldn't get the message mixed up or hear something wrong. We even got the church newsletter on email a day earlier than through the post office.

Later I entered the world of computer games. I love games and prefer the ones you can play with other people, in the living room, out in the lawn, or even riding in a car. (This would be an excellent place to put in a blurb about the game book my sister and I wrote, *Family Fun and Games*, but that wouldn't really be very professional, would it?) There aren't always other people handy to join me in a game, but the computer is sitting there, ready, willing, and able to beat me in any game that I choose. I usually choose Free Cell or hearts, but I do like rummy and even solitaire is fun.

Okay, so now I am an addict. The computer is part of my daily existence, and I am very grateful for those pests that pushed me into using it. I am happy with the way things are now. I don't want to learn any more new skills. (But I don't think I would have ever been happy having to crank a car to get it started.)

LIVING WITH THE PAST IN THE PRESENT

I recently had the experience of spending two nights in a museum. I slept in a rather narrow double bed that was several inches higher off the floor than our bed at home. My cover was an antique quilt, and there were at least seven or eight other quilts displayed in the room. One was hanging from a frame, others were folded on a quilt rack, and one was displayed in a large embroidery hoop. Pictures on the wall continued the theme from the past, and an exquisite pitcher and bowl set were placed on a nearby table. When I got ready for bed, my jean jacket and sweatshirt looked very much out of place.

Actually this was not really a named museum but a bedroom in the home of a friend who had made her guest room into this tasteful exhibit of pieces of furniture from the past. Most of the pieces had family connections and were reminders to the couple of loved ones from the past.

I came home to look at our *museum* of furniture. My parents used to say their furniture was *early Sears Roebuck*. Some of that I still have. A highchair that came from that catalog warehouse was bought for my oldest sister, Miriam. Every one of my siblings used it and every one of my children, grandchildren, and all but infant Nathan of my great-grandchildren have used it. I don't know if it qualifies as an antique, but the scars and stains above the cracked seat proclaim that it has been used.

I have a refrigerator door full of drawings, magnet gifts, and notes to myself. These represent the current period in our life. Well, there is that one note that has an unidentified telephone number on it. It has been there quite a while but we're afraid to throw it away for fear that some day we will remember whose number it is and realize that we need it.

I'm glad our bed is not high like my friend's antique one. I couldn't hide all the treasures and files of papers that I stash there if my bedcovers didn't come clear to the floor. Speaking of bedcovers, I do have several wonderful quilts that were made for us by people in churches where Lester served or from his mother and my sister. I put them on the beds only when company is coming because great-grandchildren, visiting grand-dogs, and our own cats are not always providing the best care for these heirlooms.

My aunt left Lester and me each nice pieces of walnut furniture that she had acquired for her home in Norman, Oklahoma. She had bought them and had them refinished and they now are a reminder of her good taste. I am not quite sure that they fit in with the foldout sofa bed and particleboard walls of our view room.

My mother's walnut corner china cupboard that she bought in Woodword and Lothrop Department Store in Washington graces the corner of our dining room where our mail-order table and chairs of a different wood pro-vide an eating space. Her nice dishes and glassware are displayed inside if I ever decide to use them instead of my plastic sets.

We have Lester's mother's coffee grinder on our refrigerator, a picture of my grandmother framed in the living room in a wooden oval frame, and a wonderful bookcase full of old books that a lonely man in one of our churches left for Lester. This bookcase has glass doors that lift up and slide back out of the way for easy selection of books. Some of the books are great literature. Others such as *Billy Whiskers in the South* show the racist thoughts of the past century. We keep them only for historical purposes.

These isolated pieces of possible antique worth are scattered throughout our house next to things like a computer desk loaded with printouts from the computer, inflatable toys to use in the pond if it ever gets warm enough again, and newspapers, magazines, and books we intend to read soon. If I were to pick a period our home represents, it would have to be the Now and Then Period.

Oh, I forgot to mention, we do have two very authentic antiques that have had some repairs, probably need a little refinishing, but are still pretty durable and useful. These antiques are not kept in any one place but can be found in various parts of our home at different times. They have a long family history—from both sides of our families. Like many of our other older things, they are a combination of good memories of the past, practical uses for today's living, and fit in well with the other items in the house.

These two antiques are called Lester and Carolyn. We find many uses for them each day in spite of their age. In fact, we are so fond of them that we will not pass these along to our heirs. We plan on taking them with us.

6

I DID IT MY WAY

My life has taught me lessons
That plans can wait a while,
So learn from me, relax, and try
To greet each change and smile.

FRIENDS AND NEIGHBORS

One of the best things about living in a parsonage family is experiencing all the wonderful friends and neighbors in each community where we lived. One of the worst things about living in a parsonage family is leaving all these people when it is time to move. As we followed the moving van out of the town where we have been close to so many great people, I usually cried. I felt that there would never be other neighbors as good to us as the Whipples and the Argabrights. Then we pulled into our next home and found Bill and Louise ready to share years with us as our special next-door friends. If we had not made this move, we would not have added these names to our list of those never to be forgotten.

Our denomination has a policy against a minister returning to the former church for weddings and funerals. This is to protect the new minister from having a much beloved former minister constantly darkening the doors of the church. But there is no policy that can keep us from retaining special friends from each of the places we have lived. Many of those in each congregation became good friends. A few very special people in each church will be a part of our lives forever.

An example of one such person was a widowed teacher in Lester's first church. The first Easter we were in Archie, we decided that both for economy and to set an example, I would not wear anything new to the Easter service. Our income was very limited with Lester in seminary, me home with the four children, and the small salary from the church. However, we could have squeezed out enough money for a few new things for me, but we decided against it. We knew there were some that also could not really afford new clothes, and if I went to church wearing my usual Sunday dresses, they would not feel they were out of place in their older duds.

The Tuesday following Easter I received a nice note from this tiny little lady. She said that she had noticed that I wasn't wearing anything new for Easter and felt that the minister's wife had enough sacrifices in her life that she should at least be able to have a new outfit for Easter. She enclosed a $40 check, which she instructed should be used for new clothes for me.

Forty dollars was a good amount in those days, yet I knew it would hurt her feelings if I did not do as she wished. The next Sunday I wore a new light green skirt, matching jacket, contrasting blouse, and a hat. I still had enough money left over to buy Susan a new pair of shoes.

Both Susan and I have outgrown those Easter gifts of years ago (Well, maybe I could still wear the hat if I haven't gotten too bigheaded), but I can picture each line of those clothes as well as I can those I ordered just this year.

And what is more important, I will never forget the thoughtfulness and love that this generous lady and dozens more like her showed to the wife of a new minister who was still trying to find her way in this new life.

PRECIOUS MEMORIES

Sometimes I get a little tired of all this nostalgia bit. Everywhere you go these days there are people who think the good old days were the greatest ever. I suspect that all generations felt this way to a certain extent, but we see the problems in our present times so clearly it is hard to think that they will ever be thought of with fondness.

Churches are notorious for clinging to the past. In spite of new movements for contemporary worship, there is really not that much change. In fact, when I attended such a service recently, I found myself thinking back to our nondenominational community church and Sunday School. There was not a big difference. What seems to be a new method of worship to many is a throwback in my experience to the *old time religion*. I cherish the memories of those days where neighbors led the service and the singing was lusty. However, I appreciate the present *traditional* services and give them my support.

This love affair with the past astonished my mother. I remember her comment when a neighbor was proudly showing off the big black kettle she had bought to put in her front yard. My mother said, "Why on earth would anyone want that in their yard? I couldn't wait until we got running water, and I could get rid of that big black kettle." To her the kettle was not a beautiful reminder of things past, but a backbreaking reminder of a time when things were much less pleasant.

In some popular franchise restaurants, the walls are covered with things from the past. Everyone gets sentimental when they see an old bottle of shaving lotion or a container that once held an everyday product in the kitchen. This may save the recycling centers a load, but there will have to be a limit to how much of the past we can save. The world has only a certain number of windowsills to place bottles on.

I wonder what will be treasured from our time. Will my great-grandchildren be eagerly searching my closets for an empty plastic bottle that once held Dawn dishwashing detergent? Or will my aerosol can of Right Guard be as treasured as the empty bottles of Avon are? I wonder if some future Thornton will be planting ivy in my worn-out electric blender as we now see the old coffee grinders used. Perhaps my electric skillet with the chipped leg will someday be a conversation piece on the coffee table of a future home while the residents speak softly of the good old days at the turn of the century.

And when the treasured melodies of our times are replayed on whatever machine for music is popular in the future, will my great-grandchildren get misty eyed remembering that at good old Granny's house, we used to hear that old song, "YMCA"?

When this happens, I think I will have a good laugh to think that anyone could consider the early 2000s as the Good Old Days.

HOLIDAY THOUGHTS AND MEMORIES

I am writing this on Christmas Eve. Since the church services were all canceled because of a snowstorm, and we have our groceries and last minute gifts, all I have to do tonight is wrap a few presents and relax. Of course our family is not coming en masse until Sunday, but different ones will be arriving before that. That gives me a chance to see each one a little before the whole crowd comes. I keep losing track, but I think there will be twenty-five here on Sunday. That includes one baby, two preschoolers, three school-aged, one teenager, and Lester and me as middle age plus-ers. Everyone else is between twenty and fifty-five. I figure that is the group that can do the work while I play with the six great-grandchildren. But then I was never very good at figuring, so I imagine it won't work out that way.

Some of them will still be here for New Year's Eve. We have a wild party then, with cheese and crackers, Dr. Pepper, Coke, dairy eggnog, and probably some peanuts and pretzels. Since the sleeping space for some will be the same as our playing space, we don't last too long after midnight. But we do have fun. They tease me about being low scorer in some of the card games, but I usually win in the word games, such as Boggle. Lester wins in Scrabble and chess, and we all are winners in party games in the living room.

We play anything from "I Am Somebody" to "Charades," "Murder," "Killer," to "Coffee Pot." I don't know which is my favorite game, but I know one great-grandchild's favorite game is "Hide the Thimble." I can remember when it was mine also.

Which takes me back to memories of Christmas Eve when I was a child. In the East people didn't usually put up their Christmas trees until the twenty-third or even the twenty-fourth. So sometimes our Christmas Eve was spent decorating the tree. My brother Harold, who was still single then, would go to People's Drug Store late Christmas Eve afternoon and buy all of his Christmas presents there. Then he would bring them home and have my sister Ellen and me wrap them up for him.

The mountain of gifts under the tree grew during the evening until it looked like we would never get done with the gifts in the morning. Eight kids giving to eight siblings, plus what our parents and some generous aunts gave us, made quite a pile.

I can remember how proud I was when my brother Vernon liked the tiny yellow-handled screwdriver with a pocket clip that I had selected for him. He put it in his pocket right away and seemed to be delighted with it. He should have been because it cost me ten cents to buy it for him!

Sometimes Harold would suggest that we go drive around the ritzy parts of Washington to look at the lights. Not too many people in our neighborhood did anything but have one tree in their living room. But an affluent neighborhood not too far away had homes decorated with lights on the outside. I remember one home that used just blue lights. I thought that was as pretty as any decoration could be. Another place had a silver tree in a bay window with nothing on it but red lights and red bows. That was also neat.

Now I don't use either of those ideas. It is too much fun to have the hodgepodge of decorations we have accumulated over the years. They say your home should reflect your personality. Well, at Christmas my home says I am a collector, a sentimentalist, and a bit lazy. Each year I leave off a few things that get to be too much trouble to put up again. Instead of the garlands around the windows, a new color-changing electric tree does fine. Instead of the outdoor lights, the Boy Scout wreath is enough. Decorations from church bazaars, gifts from former church members, and recordings of church Christmas programs remind us that our family is enlarged by many church congregations we have been a part of.

And Mother Nature nicely decorated the hedge outside our windows with white snow, so it is good I didn't mess up her handiwork. It still is not nice to fool with Mother Nature!

We will have a festive meal and for some of us it will be the first of the season. For others it will be the third, fourth, or in one case, fifth time to gather with a different branch of the family tree.

That's okay. It will be the first for us, so we will pretend every guest will come with a mouth watering for that turkey and ham. At least they will know I cared enough to cook it for them, even if they are already sick of it.

It is nice since Lester is retired that we can be with our family at the date that meets their schedules instead of worrying about the church's activities. It is great to have those church memories joining us along with the family events. And for the church events I usually didn't have to cook a turkey!

HOW DO YOU SPELL RELIEF?

I have just discovered another pitfall of being middle age plus. Naturally a pitfall is not a positive thing, but I have decided that anything is a positive thing if you can laugh about it. It is more fun to laugh at something when you share it, so even though my mother would not think this a proper story to tell, I can't keep it to myself any longer.

Recently my husband was going to look at the new Habitat for Humanity house site near Moundville. Although we also live near Moundville, but on the other side, I decided to ride along to see the location and get to see a part of our neighborhood that I don't often see. We found the lovely spot on a hillside overlooking a small valley. The former extension agent blood in Lester made him want to do some measuring and looking at drainage possibilities, so he was busy with his equipment and notebook for some time.

I had not taken my walk for the day, so I decided that it would be interesting to start walking back toward Moundville while he continued his work. That way I could have a new route to walk, he would not be pressured to hurry, and I would have more time when I returned home since I would have my walk out of the way. I forgot to tell you that our daughter and great-granddaughter were also with us. They both agreed that it would be fun to take the walk with me.

We were enjoying the new terrain and talking about how much different the lay of the land is just the few miles away from our home. A friendly couple in a pick-up stopped to see if we needed help, but we told him we were walking for fun. I imagine they wondered who we were and why an older woman, a little girl, and her grandmother would be out walking in his neighbor-hood. They didn't ask any questions but drove on with a friendly wave.

After walking a mile, there was still no sign of Lester coming in the car. I decided that it hadn't been a good idea for me to have enjoyed a Dr. Pepper right before we left home. The open rolling fields didn't offer many opportunities for solving my problem, and even though there were no houses in sight, I decided I would try to forget my need, knowing that Lester would soon be there.

We continued about another half mile. Still no sign of our car, but we had come to a wooded area where there was a track off the main road down the side of the adjoining field. I decided that, farm girl that I was, this was the solution.

When I mentioned what I was going to do, the great-granddaughter realized she had the same problem and wanted to accompany me. This was the first time that I realized that even though this child had been raised in a rural area, she had never use nature's restroom before. I wasn't in a mood to teach her at this point, but she soon caught on as I stepped off the path into the woods, chose my private spot, and pointed to one for her.

As a child I often didn't want to go all the way to the outhouse but made a quick stop somewhere in the backyard. On hundreds of campouts, canoe trips, and picnics, I found comfort hidden in rustic spots. This was no different, even though it had been several years since I had the experience.

I said this was no different, and it wasn't, until I tried to get up. The area I had chosen was well carpeted with low-lying stickery grasses. Hidden in the thick leaves were dozens of thorny branches. When it was time to rise, my legs wouldn't cooperate. There was nothing to push against except the sticker-infested ground. A small tree was just out of reach, so after about three tries to push up from the ground, I did a version of a duck walk, hampered by the style in which I was wearing my clothing at the time, until I reached the tree.

The tree had a vine growing around it, which I was afraid might be poison ivy, but at this point the fear of a rash was not as great as remaining in my present predicament. My daughter was waiting on the road. I knew I could call to her for help, but if we were all out of sight, then Lester wouldn't know where we were when he came with the car.

With extreme effort and using the tree as a handhold, I regained my feet and possibly some of my dignity. My leg muscles were screaming for relief as we walked back to the main road, and I was delighted to see Lester, our car, and a nice soft empty front seat I could fall into.

So much for all the pluses of being past middle age. There are some minuses too.

VIEWS FROM THE WINDOW

Our dining room table sits inside double glass doors. From this vantage point we can look out and see the activity at our bird and squirrel feeder. We can also see part of the pond and what is going on there. Recently our geese pair returned, but they were having trouble deciding which of the nests that we put up would be their home for this season. We have one of the green nests that have been manufactured just for geese to use to hatch their eggs. It has a portion cut down lower on one side so the baby goslings can drop down to the water after they hatch. But we also have a washtub, a homemade nest that Lester created the year we had two pair fighting over the green nest.

This year only one pair has shown up and one day they are *playing house* in one nest and the next day in the other. I have a feeling they will opt for the green one, but Lester thinks they'll go the washtub route. Either way it is good to have them back.

We also have an abundance of cardinal pairs using our feeders along with the winter birds that haven't left, and some mourning doves that just recently appeared to scavenge on the ground where the messy songbirds scatter the seed. Hearing the doves is a sure sign of spring for me, and just yesterday I heard the first mating calls of the doves.

A big blue heron patrols the shorelines of our pond daily to catch some of our fish for his/her(?) lunch, and today a pair of ducks stopped by. Of course, one squirrel will usually find his way to the feeder and hang by his rear feet while he robs seed from the squirrel-proof bird feeder. We don't care. He's hungry too, and he's fun to watch.

I sit at our table and observe all these beauties of nature while the television is playing in the adjoining room. I hear about the mother of all bombs, our soldiers being killed or injured by friendly fire, possible new dates for beginning a war, and the latest suicide bomber attack.

Somehow when I look outside, these news reports don't seem to be real. It's a peaceful world I am seeing and with spring coming, a few good rains, and crops in the fields, it should be a lovely day in the neighborhood. And it is. Except our neighborhood is no longer confined to what I can see from our home or to friends who live close by. Our neighborhood is the world, and it has some very ugly things going on right now.

I think back to other times when many ugly things were going on the world, and I realize that is really most of the time. World War II, the Korean and Vietnam conflicts, the Gulf War, and the Iraq War have all been sources of worry in my lifetime.

Even though I am not sure what any of these events settled for the world, I take comfort in the fact that there are still geese that return, birds that grace our feeders, and comical squirrels to entertain us.

In spite of what the human race can do to dirty our neighborhood, there are still the beauties and wonders of nature. In my middle age plus years, I will continue to believe that "this too will pass" so I can look outside and rejoice. Each spring shows me that it can continue to be a lovely day in the neighborhood.

TELLING THE STORIES IS IMPORTANT

I discovered something last weekend. I guess I knew it already, but it didn't come home to me until the weekend I spent with many members of my family. What I discovered was the fact that now I am *The Older Generation*. It really was a shock for me to realize this. For years I was the *little one*, the *youngster*, the *baby*. With seven older siblings and several very involved aunts and uncles, I never anticipated that I would some day be one of the ones to be the keeper of the family lore.

At my sister's memorial service, I was the only one of her (my) generation to be able to attend. Because of some temporary health problems the other remaining siblings weren't there. So as we sat around talking about the family, I was constantly being asked for facts. Some of these facts I didn't know or had to really think quite a while to decide the answer. Some of my nieces and nephews were telling stories of their experiences as children. Their interpretation of the actual facts of the occasion sometimes differed from my memory. Time has a way of softening memories to take away any hurt or disappointment. But it also has a way of mixing up the facts.

Memories of one occasion can blend in with a similar or different event until we are convinced that the two actions happened at the same time. Sharing thoughts helps clarify some of those confusions. Often it doesn't really matter if the facts are exactly accurate—if the feeling behind the memory is true. However, there is something in us that makes each of us want to correct a faulty memory, especially if it is someone else's memory error.

It is very interesting to see what memories these younger relatives were sharing. Most of the stories were not of dramatic events but were more of fun times doing common things. Tales of nighttime games on the lawn or stories of a family pet were shared as often as those of weddings or funerals.

There were representatives of five of the eight siblings in the Gray family sharing these memories. I was the oldest one there. I had lived in the family home with one of the parents (or grandparents) of each of those there. I was the only one who had experienced their parent as a child, teenager, or young adult.

As the questions kept coming, I began to feel the responsibility of this role. The oldest of these relatives is fourteen years younger than I am. The youngest was a ten-year-old. What I told them about our family's past would be passed on to others yet to come. Someday each of these, hopefully, will be one of *Oldest Generation*. Perhaps some of what I mentioned to them this weekend will be what they tell those who are asking them questions.

The very greatest thing about this experience is *that they were asking questions*. Too often we go our merry way, wrapped up in what we are doing each day, and let the opportunity slip by to ask questions of those who know the answers.

My husband is spending hours on genealogical research to find out things his mother could have told him easily. She didn't talk about some family members very much, and now Lester is having a hard time trying to learn more about his ancestors.

When I was younger, I never heard much about people looking for family records. Our transient, young nation was involved with going westward, finding new lands, and putting down new roots. Records weren't kept and often the family didn't even know what happened to Uncle Joe or his family. Now we have the records, the census figures, and snapshots to help us learn about our past. But none of these is as good as talking to someone who was there.

One of the responsibilities I felt as we visited was to not paint our departed loved ones with too grand a brush. Our training to not speak ill of the dead sometimes translates into making semi-gods out of older relatives. We all know that no one is perfect, and letting others know a little of the weaknesses or mistakes of an ancestor can be helpful. If we are continually judging ourselves by a fictional hero, we can easily develop a poor self-image. On the other hand, I didn't want to overdo talk about someone's lapses.

So if I am *The Older Generation* then I need to be very careful about what memories I leave behind. I sure don't want them to remember only how great I was. Maybe I should try to make a few mistakes before it is too late!

PEOPLE WHO NEED PEOPLE
ARE THE LUCKIEST PEOPLE . . .

This has been a week of renewed friendships for me. Since I have begun writing and had books published, I have enjoyed making many new friends. Folks read my work and feel they know me. We get together as old friends when we first meet. This is a wonderful privilege. All of my readers could write books about their lives, and each would be full of wonderful stories of their times and places.

We had the fun of sharing experiences with such a friend whose life is quite different from ours. Our rural backgrounds had little commonality with his big city roots. Our large families contrasted with his small one. Family histories and heritages were not at all similar. Yet with all these differences, we find pleasure in a friendship that helps us each learn more about the other's background and present life. We not only learn about the other, but we learn more about ourselves as we see ourselves through the eyes of our friend. I continue to cultivate and cherish opportunities to experience different lifestyles and backgrounds through acquaintances and friendships with those whose lives we touch.

Other friendships have been re-formed this week also. Through a Nevada friend who moved away, I became reconnected to an old college friend. At least fifty years have passed since my former housemate and I had exchanged letters, phone calls, or visits. But through the courtesy of a mutual friend, the phone system, and email, we are now caught up on each other's lives and are making plans for a personal visit soon.

Still another bonus came to me this week when I was speaking at a church in north Kansas City. Because of church friends, my sister and I had been invited to present the program for a United Methodist Women's meeting. This was fun because it caused Ellen to come over here for an overnight. We enjoy making these presentations together. When we arrived at the church, I found that six of my friends from the Savannah Church, north of Saint Joseph, had heard that I would be speaking and came down to hear the program. We had a chance, during the refreshment period, to visit together and try to cram each family's news into this short time period. Since it couldn't be done to our satisfaction, plans are underway for us to take our program up to Savannah. This will allow me to also see some special friends there who were not able to come down to the Kansas City meeting.

In addition to all these *gifts* of the week, one evening I got a phone call from a former next-door neighbor. She was sitting out on her patio where we had shared many pleasant evenings visiting with her and her late husband. She had been remembering these times, so she used her cordless phone. We had a nice talk while we were miles apart but enjoying the evening together anyway.

A pleasant luncheon with a newcomer to town, a drop-by visit from a neighbor with shared garden vegetables, and a call from a reader wanting to discuss poison ivy treatments have all added to my week. A very special moment occurred at church when a young lady who had grown up in the church, but now lives away from here, took time to come greet me personally after the service. The chance to share a brief moment and learn a little of her life made the day more special to me.

The mail brought other opportunities to remember friends as well as a reminder of an upcoming Elderhostel where I will be a leader. My topic is "Laugh Every Day," so I look forward to sharing fun moments with a roomful of new friends. If history repeats itself, there will probably be a connection through at least one of those attending to someone in my past. This happens to me quite often and reminds me that we better behave ourselves wherever we are because someone will know us or know someone who does know us.

Since some of my best friends are family members, I don't want to omit them from my pleasures of the week. Regular phone calls, emails, and personal visits from family members are such a common part of my life that I can't imagine what my life would be without them. I look forward to turning on the computer to see what message Susan has sent today. A late evening ring of the phone usually means that Mark has called to catch up on the news. The sound of the sliding door to the porch lets me know that Shirley or some of her family members are dropping by for a few minutes, and a late afternoon telephone call often comes from Michael or his wife, Jenny. Hearing the booming voice of my ninety-five-plus-year-old brother Harold's voice always amazes me, and I enjoy the wit and liveliness of sister Gertrude on the phone. Of course, Ellen and I are constantly on email making plans for our next get-together.

I like to be alone at times and love the quiet of our country home, but the joy I get through all my old and new friends makes middle age plus the very best of times.

MEMORIES ARE MADE FROM SUCH AS THIS

During this holiday season many of us middle age plus folk like to think back to the *good old days* with nostalgia and emotion. We go on and on about how great these holidays were in the past when we were children. But I am going to surprise you today. I have been marveling all this season at the great things we can enjoy this year.

For example: Mark and his family weren't coming to Missouri from Texas until later in the holiday, but on Christmas morning our daughter-in-law, Joan, used her brand new digital camera to take a picture of our son as he was unwrapping one of his presents. Then our grandson Jonathan sent it to us on his computer, so we saw this picture within minutes of when it was taken. It wasn't as good as having them here, but it made us very happy to share this way with the distant family.

Then, later in the week, they will be coming to Missouri, possibly on the same day as our daughter Susan will be driving up from Austin. Since they don't know their exact schedule and won't until they are ready to leave, they have exchanged cell phone numbers so they possibly can make connections somewhere along the road. If they do get together, then they can use these same cell phones to call back and forth between the two cars so they know when the other needs to stop for gas or other necessities.

This is a far cry from the time Lester and I were driving to a Thornton reunion in Colorado in a two-car caravan with Lester's brother Paul. We took a wrong turn in Wichita and never got back together again until we reached the aunt's home in Colorado. This caused Lester's mother a lot of worry for she was sure that the other car must be having trouble, or we would have seen them somewhere along the way.

Car trouble is another thing that isn't as worrisome as in the past. Again we can whip out our cell phone and call for help instead of getting out to walk for help. I am reminded of the time I was returning to Archie from visiting my mother in the hospital here in Nevada. Eighteen-month-old Susan was asleep in the back seat of my parent's car that I was driving. Since I didn't know that their fuel gauge didn't work properly, I ran out of gas just north of Butler. It was drizzling rain but I had no choice but to wake Susan up and start carrying her as I walked up the road toward a distant house. Thankfully two women in a car spotted the stalled car and then saw me walking with the child. They stopped to offer help. A dozen cars had already passed by without stopping, but these kind women did stop. In fact, they drove me to Passaic to get some gas and then drove me back to the car and waited until they were sure the car would start. These were complete strangers to me. But by coincidence they were members of the Passaic United Methodist Church that Lester later served as a minister, along with the Ohio Street Church in Butler. I reminded them of their kind act when we met again years later. They had nearly forgotten the incident. But I never will forget the joy I felt when they stopped. A cell phone would have eased my problem back in 1964. But then I would not have known the helpfulness of these two women, would I?

During the recent big snowfall I was against a deadline to get my article for the "Senior Page" into the newspaper office. Without leaving my home, I was able to write the article, send it into the newspaper office through my computer, and then fax the hard copy to the office as a backup. I didn't leave the house, get my feet cold or wet, or risk driving on the snow.

When I first started writing for the paper, I used an electronic typewriter, which I thought was about as helpful as any machine could be. I could erase a word or a letter and start over without using White Out (which was a great advancement when it first was available) or typing something over again. I remember some of the copy I sent in with pencil marks and arrows showing that I wanted a sentence or a paragraph put into another place. Now that can be done with one or two strokes of my trusty mouse. The only trouble with this is that if there is an error, it is probably mine and I can't blame it on someone else.

My car tells me when I am running out of gas, when a door is ajar, or if there is a problem in the engine. It turns on my headlights, whether I want them on or not, and turns them off a minute or so after I park the car and leave. My battery never runs down because of a light being left on overnight, but then I can never sneak up on anyone with no headlights on. That is not a big problem, but I do like to drive without them on our country road when there is a full moon so I can see how bright the moon really is.

The memories I pass on about today's good old days will include thankfulness for many of the things that were not even dreamed of in my childhood—or even in my middle aged years. But I still will cherish those from the 1930s and 1940s. No matter what each year offers, there are pleasant memories to cherish.

PREACHERS' KIDS

Every minister who is a parent has the problem of dealing with the image of the *Preacher's Kids. P.K.s*, as they are often called, can be angelic or devilish. Most of them are a healthy mixture of the two. However, in smaller communities they often receive an undeserved reputation or, on the opposite end, get overlooked for opportunities.

In our first two parsonages, our family fitted into a neighborhood of other children and active families. We had many friends and good neighbors. But I never had to worry about what our own kids were doing, because I would be told several times a day if they were doing anything that wasn't considered safe, polite, or legal. The saying, "It takes a village to raise a child," was converted into, "It takes a congregation to raise a P.K."

I remember one time Michael and another young teen in the church were having a snowball fight in front of the church. This congregation had the happy habit of standing around outside after the service was over to visit a while. Most of the people had drifted to their cars when the two boys found the remains of a late spring snowbank and began their playful fight. Michael ran up the steps to the church to get a better position when his friend aimed a ball at him. Michael ducked; the ball hit the ancient church door and the wood cracked open. A temporary patch took care of the problem for some time. Now there is a beautiful new door at the entrance, but the story is still told about the Preacher's Kid that ruined the old door.

In two schools our children were not given a spot on the basketball team or allowed to play a hard-to-learn instrument in the band. We were actually told that the reason for the choice was because "The Preacher's Kids won't be here very long, so the position should go to someone who is a permanent resident." (In both cases our child remained in that school for five or six more years.)

Through the years our friendship with other parsonage families has shown that some of their children go through a semi-rebellious stage in college—or maybe in the later years of high school. Regardless of how nice the adults in town have treated them, their peers have sometimes given them a hard time. They did not get invited to a certain party because the other youth were afraid the *minister* would find out. This was probably a blessing, but the kids themselves didn't see it that way at the time. Sometimes they felt they had to show their peers that they were just as worldly as anyone.

Looking back on these experiences from adulthood, Preachers' Kids seldom have any hard feelings about their lives. Many second and third generations of ministers have been raised in parsonages, and even if they kicked up their heels for a while in early adulthood, they settled in to being very good ministers. However, there are also some that have put their lives of expected Sunday School and church attendance behind them and found their *calling* in other fields.

Some benefits do exist that are appreciated. Tuition at church colleges is usually reduced for Preachers' Kids. Opportunities to mingle with people of different races, economic conditions, and geographical areas help them have a broader concept of the world than some children can experience. And at church camps, youth retreats, and mission tours they can share stories with other P.K.s.

One of my favorite stories comes from a Disciples of Christ minister who had himself been a P.K. growing up in a small town. When his children were criticized for some action and a church member implied it was because of their being P.K.s, our friend had a good reply. "The reason Preachers' Kids misbehave is that they have to play with the deacons' children all of the time!"

OUR CHILDREN SPEAK FOR THEMSELVES

Throughout this book I have described incidents involving one or all of our four children. It occurred to me that I should let them each speak for themselves. They could express their feelings of being a son or daughter of a minister better than I ever could.

When I emailed them with my request, I got responses such as, "Homework again!!" However, they each quickly sent me the following essays.

Since each of our children is quite different, each child had a different experience. But many of the things they report are very similar.

It was a joy for Lester and me to read these reports, and we feel honored to be able to include them along with my memories.

In their own words, meet Michael, Shirley, Mark, and Susan—P.K.s who enhance the name of Preachers' Kids.

I WAS STEREOTYPED
Michael H. Thornton

The first move from Nevada to Archie wasn't very painful for me. At eleven I didn't have a lot of close friends where we had been living since we lived out of town. We were moving to a newer house and there were many things that I hadn't done before. Baseball, basketball, and other sports were big for me. I also got to join Boy Scouts.

On the negative side I got the first taste of *P.K.* I was stereotyped as either a goodie or as a bad kid depending on who was talking (a little old lady or my peers). Many times I found myself trying to prove that I was the same as all the other kids. We stayed in Archie for six years and I became very comfortable there.

The next move was painful for me in many ways. I was moved between my junior and senior years in high school, which wasn't *fair*. I also had to move away from the friends that I had. Although I did make new friends in Butler, I was resentful for some time.

Overall, I didn't feel resentment for Dad on his choice and the move. It was just the process. (When I grew up and had my own children, I made a point to stay in one place while they were growing.)

I think that the two moves that I made did help later on. I was better equipped to handle new places and new people. I wasn't involved in the later moves except to help physically move the belongings. I was on my own and didn't get the same impact. It was somewhat different to go home for a visit when I hadn't lived there.

One thing that helped keep us centered was the fact of The Wayside, my mother's family's home farm. We always knew that it was there and eventually would become the *home* again.

Overall I did not become *scarred for life* by the experience. It probably helped me mature and handle experiences as an adult somewhat better.

I WAS DEALT A DOUBLE WHAMMY
Shirley Garnett

I was almost nine when we moved to Archie, Dad's first church. At Archie, I was dealt a double whammy by the kids at school. I was the *new kid* and also a *preacher's kid*. The kids did not accept me easily. I was forced to be more extroverted. I didn't have many friends. There was one main friend at school and we were always together. Her name was Shirley also. In addition, there were some neighborhood kids I played with and I had a few friends from the church, some my age and some adults. I joined the church at Archie, sang in the choir, and was involved in 4-H. I was chosen to attend State 4-H Club Week when I was almost fifteen. The day I left to go to the 4-H Club Week, we lived in Archie. When I came back we lived in Butler. The family had moved to Dad's second church while I was gone.

In Butler, the kids were more accepting of me. I was forced again to be more extroverted. I met several friends in Butler, some from the church, both adults and peers, and a few at the high school. My first day in high school I was again the *new kid* in school, but by then I had gotten used to being a *preacher's kid*, so it wasn't as big an ordeal. My first class in high school was band. My second class was chorus/gym, where I met my best friend, who later became my sister-in-law. My third class was biology, where I met my future husband.

After graduating from high school, I went to Central Methodist College to become a teacher. At college I experienced a different angle to being a *preacher's kid*. Many of the kids in college were also *P.K.s*. While in college, I felt a part of the group, not just on the edge.

At the time of Dad's next church move, I stayed in Butler with my husband and baby. It was hard for me to go to church when I knew I wouldn't see Dad in the pulpit. I brought my children up in the church. Penny was active in the youth group, and I also was involved and went on work camp trips to the Ozark Methodist Manor for several years. As a team member, I was supposed to write a short article on my ideas of the themes for the work camp. I would like to include one of those articles I wrote over the years of service to the church.

CIRCLE OF CARE

I had an experience in early childhood where I had to completely trust, depend, and lean on my family. I had both eyes operated on at the same time. I had patches on both eyes for quite a while. My family had to do everything for me. I couldn't see anything. They had to lead me by the hand everywhere I went. I had to be fed. My family has always been important to me.

ENRICHED BY THE EXPERIENCE OF DAD'S CALL
Mark Thornton

I don't really remember the exact details of how I first knew of Dad's call, but I do have recollections of a vague sense of anxiety on Mom's part. We would be moving, of course, and that meant she'd be an hour away from her aging parents. I'm sure there was concern about the impact of a change in schools and circumstances on the children. But, I sensed those issues weren't the real cause of worry. Rather, I think there was concern for the future of the family.

We all approached the move with a positive attitude. For me, it was a move from a fairly isolated existence on the farm to living in a town with social opportunities all around. I know my childhood was more full and enjoyable as a result of the changes. And the timing for me was to enter first grade at the same time as all the other children (there was no kindergarten in this school), so I was no more new than the rest of my class.

However, because it was a very small town (although at the time, it didn't seem so small), everyone knew I was the preacher's kid. This led to some teasing, but in my case, it was infrequent and never really bothered me. I was aware that for my older brother, Michael, it sometimes did cause pain from peer pressure.

But for me, the earliest memory of being the minister's son came in the form of a sermon. I think I was in second grade at the time. The evening before, the family had been returning from a car trip when we came upon the scene of a horrible accident just north of Archie, our home at the time. As we passed, I made a comment about "I hope it's no one we know . . ." We soon heard that it was. The Swigert family had been hit head on—too common in those days of two-lane roads. They ran the local drug store, were in our church, and Mike, a year younger than me, was the only survivor.

The next day in church, I was sitting listening with my typical disinterested mode to my father's sermon, when I heard him relate the incident, and my comment, without attribution. The sermon went on to point out that we should care for our fellow man, and that we should mourn and pray for those affected by tragedies, regardless of whether we know them or not. I don't recall the details, but I suspect the *Good Samaritan* or similar Biblical examples may have been used. I do remember being profoundly shamed—and sorry. To this day, I can't see a car accident without wondering whose lives were impacted, and how surviving family members must feel. I know that Mike Swigert was changed by that night, and I think I was by the next morning.

The summer between my sixth and seventh grades, the church moved us to Butler, a much larger, but small, town. I was again blessed by the timing of joining classmates going from elementary to junior high and was excited by the opportunities of living in a town with things to do. I was at the age when you become very concerned about how others perceive you. This was the first time I recall being uncomfortable about my father's profession. I was sometimes teased about being the preacher's kid with comments like, "You can't say/do that, you're the preacher's kid."

This led to another memory of being the subject of a sermon. I was with a group of kids my age at the city park in the same block as the parsonage. We were playing tennis, badly, and there was a lot of banter back and forth across the net between two doubles teams. Somewhere as the insults progressed, a comment was made that I couldn't say any curse words, because I was the preacher's kid. I, of course, took the challenge and went on to show that I was quite fluent in the use of profanity—and could illustrate the point. I purposely used every bad word I could think of and strung them together in a sentence that would have made a sailor on shore leave proud. At exactly the same time as I started the sentence, my mother, on an evening walk, came alongside the tennis courts and heard every bit of my speech.

She never said a word to me about it. But the next Sunday, there was a sermon I remember. I was in the choir, which was behind my father's pulpit, so that I could not see his face as he spoke. But, as he talked about the degrading effect of profanity and how we all have a social obligation to keep our discussions in civil terms and tones, I knew what the catalyst for the sermon was. I was not actually embarrassed by the incident or sermon. I was just doing what I had to do to succeed in being accepted in my particular society.

I met quite a few preachers' kids over the years and think that planned bad behavior is a fairly common coping mechanism. There were even times that adults would say things like "You know preachers' and teachers' kids are always the worst" with a conspiratorial wink, and there seemed to be wide acknowledgment that some rebellion against strict morals was normal. I tended to mistrust any preacher's kid that didn't have a bit of a wild streak—they must not be *normal*.

Now that I'm an adult, I can look back and see how there were many other ways that my upbringing as the son of clergy has impacted me. I was exposed early and often to other religions— and other ways of thinking. I was taught tolerance and acceptance. I have engaged in stimulating discussions with friends raised in other religions as we explored beliefs. I saw parents who sacrificed personal gain for the greater good. We didn't have a lot of money, but I learned a solid work ethic. A big part of my self-image is rooted in the idea that I try to be good.

I saw that *churches* were run by people, and that, like any human institutions, there are politics involved. I was aware that religion can sometimes be used as a weapon, and righteous people can rationalize some very harmful practices in the name of God. Although I dislike those factors, I accept them as part of the process. My parents' political skills were well honed by the necessities of the job, so that I have benefited in my career from a lifetime of observation of good people skills in daily interactions.

Although as an adult, I'm not what most would describe as *religious*, I think I have a greater sense of wonder and curiosity about the human condition, the universe, and how it all came to be than most. I am sure that exposure to the core questions of belief, faith, and God in my childhood will be part of my entire life. I didn't choose to be a preacher's kid, but I wouldn't choose any other way to grow up now if I had it to do over again.

Mom didn't need to worry. The family was only enriched by the experience of Dad's call.

Growing Up P.K.
Susan Thornton

What was it like growing up as a preacher's kid? In many ways it was just like growing up as anybody's kid, but there were differences that my siblings and I experienced. And I think my experience of the P.K. phenomenon differs slightly even from my two older brothers and my sister because I was the only child who lived my entire life as the child of a minister. The others were ages eleven, nine, and six when Dad made his decision, so they knew life as normal kids before that. Their lot was to make the transition, which seemed to be difficult for them in reverse proportion to their ages, logically. They had to learn the special social skills required to make Dad's stay in the current pulpit as easy as possible after they had already known a life relatively free of these kinds of worries. Before, they could say whatever they wanted to, within reason, in Sunday School just like anybody else. Shortly after the move to his first church, experience taught them otherwise. When my sister made a statement in a youth group about Dad's beliefs, it was not appreciated when it was later circulated in different circles. Dad wound up with some *splainin* to do.

I never had to learn such lessons the hard way, because I was born into it, taken home from the hospital to a parsonage. The special traits of *P.K.ism* are innate in me. This aspect of my personality is both good and bad, but I would say that, for the most part, growing up in a minister's family was fortuitous for me. I certainly haven't felt that way all of my life. I do acknowledge that parts of it may not have much in the way of redeeming qualities (the amount of time I spent in church basements has yet to reveal its meaning or usefulness to me, for example), but I think in most ways I was blessed by the experience.

Being born in a parsonage, especially when your father is a new young minister, is a good start. People are just inclined to dote on you, especially if you live in a very small town. I have many memories of my preschool years, and I remember an abundance of love, which I just took for granted, as the way the world naturally was. When people saw us at school or town functions, they were very good to us, they had us over for delicious, old-time dinners and homemade ice cream, and we lived in a neighborhood full of kids and more nice people, with *the country* just across the road. With my oldest brother in charge, we were safe to go the few blocks to downtown where many members of the congregation and other townspeople always greeted us warmly. The only thing I remember really disliking, other than the unfairness of the rule that girls can't spit, was having to get up to go to Sunday School. But I got special treatment on Saturday nights, with extra songs from Mommy, in an effort to get me to bed early enough that I wouldn't be a grouch. But I liked church, once I got there and awake. Everybody knew me and was glad to see me, took time to talk to me and fuss over me. After the hymns and collection, I could cuddle up on the pew next to Mommy and nap, hearing my father's comforting voice coming from the front. Sometimes he would get emotional, and I would be confused, but Mommy always reassured me, maybe providing butterscotch distraction, and I'd sink back into her side. I can't think of a safer, more secure, and sounder environment to spend those crucial first years in. If my father weren't a minister, I probably would have been a farm girl. I don't know. But I know I wouldn't trade those first years for anything.

I didn't always feel that way about it. The second church, where we stayed almost the whole time I was in grade school, was in a much bigger town–4,000 people!–where the world suddenly got a little rougher and the center of attention shifted away from me. Sometimes there, when I felt overwhelmed, I would fantasize about living in the country and having animals, and I'd wish I could be a farm girl and just could not understand why my dad could have ever given up living like they did on *Lassie*!

Still, a big part of being a preacher's kid is adapting to change and new requirements. I think I was the right age to start doing that. I don't remember ever getting much ribbing or teasing about being a P.K. It didn't seem that strange; there were lots of churches with friends who were also P.K.s in that town. But as I progressed through elementary school, the unspoken demands of the role became increasingly apparent. I was in the choir, of course; an acolyte, of course; and in the Christmas play, of course. My siblings were role models, singing and playing instruments *solo*! How they could do that, I couldn't imagine. I'd get extremely self-conscious just standing a little taller than the rest of the kiddie choir. But, of course, I did it. As I grew older and Mom needed someone to be the narrator of the latest skit she'd had to write, I did even more, to help her as much as I could, though it usually scared me. We moved again, after my fifth grade year, and at that third church, I assumed more responsibilities in the youth group and even singing tenor in the choir because there weren't enough boys to fill the parts. By the time I was a teen, there were many times I would really have preferred not to go to MYF and especially not to be an officer or go to a retreat. But I did, not from any fear of reprisal from my parents, but because of the understanding my mother had given us that we were all in it together and that our actions had an impact on the whole family. I'm not saying that I understood that concept perfectly all the time, but I wanted to be as helpful to my parents and to my father's career as my older siblings had been, or at least to not harm anything. It was important to be respectful to people at the front door, because you never knew who they might be. It was important to get phone messages right and to use good etiquette when visiting another's home. No one ever really told me any of these things; I just learned by watching my family. I was put into many new situations and met many people, even foreigners, but I watched my elders until I gained a little poise and presence of my own. Those experiences have served me well in later life—in the academic, business, and real worlds.

Other parts of growing up in a minister's family were less conducive to my understanding and conducting myself in the larger world once I reached it. I'm a little ashamed to admit that the common reality of paying rent or having a mortgage payment came as a little bit of a shock to me. I certainly knew the churches had owned our homes. I'd cleaned up my room for many a visit from the trustees or bemoaned the fact that we couldn't just choose our own kitchen flooring or paint a room and be done with it instead of waiting for a committee decision. But somehow the fact eluded me that my comfortable middle-class lifestyle didn't include this key expense incurred by my friends' families. I was also basically ignorant of business in general. Mom had to work for most of my school years, but even her jobs were predominantly social work, both government and private-sector supported, so my experience of work and making money was pretty much limited to the helping fields. Since I had learned the adaptive and social skills I mentioned before, this ignorance wasn't a major stumbling block for me, however, and I am inordinately proud of the good work and good feelings my parents have created with their years of toil. I understand and can function well in the outside world now, but I often yearn for work with the meaning I know that theirs has almost always had for them.

I say "almost always" because another negative in my upbringing was watching my mother's frustrations when she had to endure periods when she couldn't find personal meaning in her work, or otherwise, due to our moves and subsequent *outsider* status in some of the later towns my dad served. I think the lowest point was in that third town when I was in junior high. She had been moved away once more from people she dearly loved, her oldest three children included, to find a town with limited possibilities for someone of her talents and a church expecting a carbon copy of the previous minister's wife. She hung on, worked for the sheriff, substitute taught, gave out samples at a church member's grocery store and the like, until she found a job in a neighboring town where she could again be of service, use her gifts, and be among people who appreciated her. But during the time when she was low, I was angry at my dad for moving her, and us, around. I found out more about the story of that first move before I was born, away from her elderly parents, and I realized that she'd been *sad* when I was little too. I had spent a lot of time at the neighbors' houses when I was a preschooler not just because they adored me. Mommy was just worn out: taking care of four kids, two dogs, two cats, birds, and fish; typing Daddy's church bulletins and school work; learning to be a proper minister's wife; and hauling me the forty-five miles by car or bus down to take care of her parents as frequently as she could, at least biweekly. To her credit, I had to figure all this out for myself. Only once, much later after I was pretty much grown, did she ever admit that she had a few resentments about it all. As we were growing up, I never heard her complain directly about Dad's choices. Her role frequently was to help me see his side too.

Mom wasn't the only one with frustrations. It wasn't much fun to watch my father be criticized and underappreciated, either. As a teenager, I became cynical and disdainful of the hypocrisy I felt was prevalent in certain sectors of the congregation. No matter what church we were in or how hard we tried, there was always a small group that didn't like Dad much, for whatever reason—his theology, his preaching, or his choice of hymns or the cars we drove. My father is a sincere and straightforward person and to see him beaten down by petty politics fueled my youthful righteous indignation. I also had a Sunday School teacher in my later teens whose theology was not as merciful as it should have been, in my opinion, so I started getting mysterious Sunday morning illnesses in order to avoid going to church altogether. I knew Dad was disappointed, but nobody forced me to go when I started not wanting to. The only time it was an issue was one morning when I decided I could mow the lawn while it was early (for me) and still cool. A church member happened to see me, since the parsonage was only two blocks down the street from the church. She tore into my dad about his child working so publicly on a Sunday, during church hours! Of course, she was right. I'd been thoughtless, but I was angry about her nosiness getting me in trouble for quite a while . . . until one evening when she came to the house to tell me that my father was in the hospital. She was the one person who was kind enough to, first, realize that I would be coming home from basketball practice unaware of a crisis in my family and, then, to get out in the cold with her bad feet to make sure I would be all right. Experiences like that began to show me that even the vocally critical folks in the church were basically good, a fact that my dad emphasized if I ever voiced my own criticisms. It took me a while, but I learned tolerance—that, as Dad told me, most people are doing their best, if I just give them the same chance I expect for myself.

These critically important lessons about our shared humanity are the most precious benefits of my P.K. experience for me today. At the time, I thought it was cool that we got to go first at potluck suppers, that our second house had a park right behind us, that my brother and I got to figure out the theme from *Close Encounters* on a pipe organ, and that we got tons of free food at Christmas. Those were certainly part of the fun. There was always something going on, loads of friends, and good, clean activity—Heaven for a child.

But I think the greatest lesson that being the lucky baby of a preacher and his gifted wife taught me is that service to others is the true path to self-contentment in adulthood. I might have had moments when I wished my parents weren't so busy, attention glutton that I am, but I know now that I am among the fortunate few. I watched my parents publicly try to live their values and beliefs, working hard to stay true to their ideals through frustrations and sometimes painfully lonely relocations. I saw them take the world of ideas seriously and without judgment—reading, thinking, writing, and sharing their thoughts openly, with warm curiosity and a sincere desire to learn and do better, but thinking no less of those who believed differently. And I witnessed their constant attempts to bring their ideals of duty and service into reality, with much success.

At Mom and Dad's fiftieth wedding anniversary, my husband was taken aback at the distances the large number of people had traveled to come help them celebrate, and he was greatly impressed at the way my siblings and I worked the crowd, as he termed it. He commented that it was beautiful to watch. Each of us instinctively made the rounds, thanking our former neighbors and forever friends for coming to our family's festive day. He said he didn't believe there was a hand to be shaken that went overlooked, and knowing us, he knew our interest and concern were genuine.

That's what it's like to be a preacher's kid. You grow up with whole communities watching over you, loving you, expecting a lot from you, remembering you long after you've moved away. You feel somewhat stifled and embarrassed by it, but you grow into it. And you become a good person who believes that others are also good and worthy of love, respect, and care. It's a fine life, all in all, and a gift I feel confident that we are each now profoundly grateful to have been given so freely and abundantly throughout our formative years. I know I am.

I BELONG

Even if there were no issue of faith, belief, or commitment to a religion, belonging to a church is one of the best feelings there is. A certain congregation can have deep emotional meaning for a person. It is a place where people care about you, know your needs, and will share in your joys and sorrows.

At a time of a death in the family, the church is an anchor to keep things steady. Even if you do not know the new minister, even if you have dropped off in your attendance, and even if you have failed to contribute financially, the church will be there for you.

Those who have not experienced the comfort of belonging to a congregation cannot realize what they are missing. When I am present at a Communion service where the members go forward to receive the elements, I feel a sense of closeness to each one as I watch them go up the aisle. I am flooded with memories of this one's kindness and that one's wit. I smile as I see the young dads juggling a baby in their arms and remember when they were some of the ones being led by the hand not too long ago.

It is like a family reunion with the longtime friends and members mixed in with the newer ones. As I watch the people pass, it is as if I am seeing the past and future parading past me. This gives me a strong sense of security, freedom, and love.

Lester has often said that it is nearly impossible to be a solitary Christian. The strength we get from each other binds us together and enriches each one of us individually.

But it goes beyond our individual congregation—and even beyond our denomination. Those who have made a commitment to a church have a special bond with all others who have done so. I now feel at home in any place of worship in spite of starting out feeling like an outsider.

The main thing that has made a difference for me is the people: the people in each of the congregations that Lester served; the people in the other churches in the communities where we lived; the men and women across our state and nation who dedicate themselves to the mission of the church; and especially the wonderful women in hundreds of United Methodist Women's units around the world have all become a part of me. I am a different person because of them.

I have become a leader where I once was afraid to even be a participant. I can serve with joy where once I hated the thought of serving. I can say that we have a better life than we would have had if Lester had not answered his call. And I can say now that I do belong.

I think I got the hang of being a minister's wife.

THE END